Options Trading Crash Course

The Most Complete Guide for Beginners With Easy-To-Follow Strategies for Creating a Powerful Passive Income Stream in 2020 Using Options

Mark Robert Rich

© **Copyright 2020 Mark Robert Rich - All rights reserved.**

The content contained within this book may not be reproduced, duplicated, or transmitted without direct written permission from the author or the publisher.

Under no circumstances will any blame or legal responsibility be held against the publisher, or author for any damages, reparation, or monetary loss due to the information contained within this book. Either directly or indirectly.

Legal Notice:
This book is copyright protected. This book is only for personal use. You cannot amend, distribute, sell, use, quote, or paraphrase any part, or the content within this book, without the consent of the author or publisher.

Disclaimer Notice:
Please note the information contained within this document is for educational and entertainment purposes only. All effort has been executed to present accurate, up to date, and reliable, complete information. No warranties of any kind are declared or implied. Readers acknowledge that the author is not engaging in the rendering of legal, financial, medical, or professional advice. The content within this book has been derived from various sources. Please consult a licensed professional before attempting any techniques outlined in this book.

By reading this document the reader agrees that under no circumstances is the author responsible for any losses, direct or indirect, which are incurred as a result of the use of the information contained within this document, including, but not limited to, —errors, omissions, or inaccuracies.

Table of Content

Introduction 11
    Financial freedom 11
    Signs of Financial Slavery 11
    Financial Freedom — What Is It and Why Do Only A Few People Have It 14
    Habits and Mindset of the Financially Free 16
    Trading Options to Gain Financial Freedom 18
    What You Will Learn in This Book 19

Chapter 1: Options Trading Basics 21
    What Are the Options? 21
        Option 21
        Derivative Contract 22
        Securities 22
        Agreed-Upon Price 23
        Specified Period 23
    Options vs. Stocks 23
    Types of Trading Options 25
        Call Option 25
        Put Option 27
    Benefits of Trading Options 28
    Disadvantages of Trading Options 30
    Tips for Getting Started With Options Trading 31
    Chapter Summary 35

Chapter 2: How Options Prices are Determined 37
The Value of the Asset 37
The Intrinsic Value 37
The Time Value 38
Volatility 39
Interest Rates 40
Dividends 41
Option Pricing Models 41
    The Black Scholes Model 42
    Binomial Option Pricing Model 43
    Monte Carlo Simulations 44
A Final Word on Pricing 44
Chapter Summary 44

Chapter 3: Basic Options Strategies Going Long 46
Going Long vs. Going Short 46
Simple Going Long Strategies 47
    Long Call 48
    Long Put 49
Chapter Summary 50

Chapter 4: Covered Call Strategy (or Protected Puts) 52
What Is a Covered Call? 52
Benefits of Covered Call Options 54
The Risks Associated with Covered Call Options 54
How to Create a Covered Call Option 55
How the Covered Call Works 55
    The Stock Price Goes Down 55

The Stock Price Does Not Change or Goes Up Slightly	56
The Stock Goes Above the Strike Price	56
Chapter Summary	56
Chapter 5: Strangles and Straddles	**58**
Types of Volatility	58
The Strangle Strategy	61
The Short Strangle	61
The Long Strangle	63
The Straddle Strategy	64
The Short Straddle	64
The Long Straddle	65
Chapter Summary	66
Chapter 6: Credit and Debit Spreads	**67**
Credit Spreads vs. Debit Spreads	67
Credit Spreads	67
How Credit Spreads Work	67
Types of Credit Spreads	68
Pros and Cons of Credits Spreads	71
Debit Spreads	71
How Debit Spreads Work	71
Types of Debit Spreads	73
Pros and Cons of Debit Spreads	76
Legging Spreads	77
What is Legging?	77
Benefits of Legging	77
How to Use Legging	78

The Risks of Legging 79

Chapter Summary 79

Chapter 7: Iron Condor 82

Benefits of the Iron Condor Spread 83

Risks of the Iron Condor Spread 84

Chapter Summary 84

Chapter 8: Selling Naked Options 85

Naked Call Options 85

Naked Put Option 86

Elements of a Naked Option 87

Benefits of Naked Options 88

Chapter Summary 88

Chapter 9: Rolling Out Options 89

How to Roll Out an Option 89

Rolling Up 89

Rolling Down 91

Rolling Forward 92

The Benefits of Rolling Out 93

Chapter Summary 93

Chapter 10: Top Trader Mistakes to Avoid in Options Trading 95

Mistake #1—Not Having a Trading Plan to Fall Back On .. 95

Mistake #2—Choosing the Wrong Expiration Date for Options 96

Mistake #3—Not Factoring In the Volatility of the Financial Market 97

Mistake #4—Not Having a Sound Exit Plan 98

Mistake #5—Not Being Flexible 99

Mistake #6—Trading Illiquid Options........................... 99

Mistake #7—Not Factoring In Upcoming Events........... 100

Mistake #8—Waiting Too Long To Buy Back Short Strategies 101

Mistake #9—Getting Legged Out Of Position 101

Mistake #10—Trading Options on Complicated Assets without First Doing Proper Research 102

Chapter Summary 102

Chapter 11: The Options Trader Mindset 104

The Traits of a Successful Options Trader 104

Dream Big 107

Chapter Summary 109

Chapter 12: Trading with LEAPS 110

Best Strategies for Using LEAPs 111

Benefits of LEAPS 112

Disadvantages of LEAPS... 113

Tips for Getting the Most Out Of LEAPS 113

Chapter Summary 114

Conclusion 116

Trading Options for Financial Freedom 117

Are You Ready To Be An Options Trader? 117

My Final Words 119

Glossary of Terms 121

From The Same Author.. 130

Introduction

Financial freedom

Many people seek it but few have it. That is because the secrets behind obtaining it are closely guarded by those who have it. This book is about exposing one true and reliable way that you can earn the financial security and independence you need to take control of the way you live your daily life.

Signs of Financial Slavery

The first active step needed to get started on a journey to financial freedom is acknowledging that you are not financially stable or free. This is a hard pill for some people to swallow and so, they avoid acknowledging it even with the overwhelming evidence to support the state.

Facing this fact is not about demeaning your integrity or bring you down. It is about giving you a foundation to start with so that you can build the financial security you need. This knowledge is needed to show you where you currently stand financially and what your resources are so that you can develop a plan to get where you need and want to be.

The following conditions are those that chain many people to financial slavery:

- **Living paycheck to paycheck.** People who live this way do not have an emergency fund and typically have accompanying credit card debt because they need to subsidize their expenses, which are higher than their income. Many people live this way. In fact, more than 40% of American households could not cover a $400 expense such as medical bills or car repairs if it came up unexpectedly in 2017.
- **Not having enough saved up to sustain their lifestyle if they were to lose their job.** People such as these do not have enough money accumulated to take time away from working daily. This is the reason why most people are in careers and jobs that bring them no joy. They need the salary to keep a roof over their heads and food in their belly and so, they deal with the circumstances that make them unhappy.
- **Not being able to pursue the activities and adventures that bring happiness while still saving and accumulating wealth.** These types of people are stuck in a cycle of trading their daily hours for money while still being unable to enjoy the money that they earn because it is not enough to allow them this enjoyment and still pay the bills.
- **Having inflexible schedules.** Most people are stuck in a cycle of working every day and going home to come back to work the next day. They have to give this time

to earn an income and therefore, become chained to their jobs.
- **Not being able to retire comfortably at the desired age.** The world over, the average age for retirement is 65 years old. However, many people are not expected to live even 20 years passed that age. That does not live much time to enjoy a life free of accumulating wealth. The sadder fact is most people do not retire with enough money saved up to enjoy the things that they want after retirement. Some others still have to work a job even after this age to sustain themselves. People who are financially free can retire at the age that they want rather than one that is dictated by someone else. They also have the capital available to do the things they want to do and still have income coming to them on a more passive basis.
- **Spending more money than earned.** This results because people want to live the lifestyle that they want but cannot afford or people needing to subsidize their income to cater to their needs. To build wealth, you cannot have more money going out than coming in. Signs that your spending exceeds your income include having a budget based on your salary, having an expense list that exceeds your net income, carrying a balance on your credit card, having rent or mortgage that is more than 30% of your net income and buying things to impress or keep up with other people.

Are you slave to your finances? Would you like to use your time in other ways while still earning a steady and growing income? Can you use an extra income to develop the lifestyle you want?

If you answer is yes to any of these income questions or relating to even just one of the conditions stated above means you can use the advice and strategies outlined in this book.

Financial Freedom — What Is It and Why Do Only A Few People Have It

Having financial freedom is more than just having a 6-month emergency fund saved up and your debt cleared. Financial freedom means taking control of your time and finances so that you can do the things that you want to do rather than what your bank account figure dictates. Being financially free means you do not need to trade your time for money.

To be able to gain this financial freedom, you need to have financial security. Financial security is the condition whereby you support the standard of living you want now and in the future by having stable sources of income and other resources available to you. That means not living paycheck to paycheck. It means not having to worry about where your next dollar will come from. It means having a huge weight lifted off your shoulders because you know there are resources you can leverage to get the things that you want and need.

People who have financial freedom are also financially independent. Financial independence is the state of having personal wealth to maintain the lifestyle and the standard of living you want without actually having to trade your daily hours for money. The assets and resources you have generated will gain that income for you so that your income remains far greater than your expenses. In essence, being financially independent means you can go for a prolonged period without trading time for money and still have the standard of living that you want. That you can go on a year-long vacation and still be secure in the knowledge that your wealth is still growing.

To be financially independent, you have to have:

- An emergency fund that can sustain your lifestyle for an extended period (years).

- Assets that produce income for you on a daily, weekly, monthly, and yearly basis.
- Very little or zero debt.

Very few people on the planet are financially secure and independent. In fact, more than 1 billion people live in extreme poverty. In 2015, it was estimated that more than 10% of the global population lived on less than US$1.90 per day.

Despite these statistics, there is hope. This hope comes from the fact that this statistic goes down every year. In fact, in 2019 less than 8% of the global population lived in extreme poverty. This is largely attributed to the fact that people being more educated about their options and are not just accepting of these poor circumstances.

Despite this improvement, most of the global population still trades their time for an hourly wage. The income earned from this is not sustainable nor will it allow them to live the standard of life that they would like. They will not be able to retire comfortably. There is no power or security in living this way.

People who are financially free have learned and harnessed the power of passive income. Passive income is wealth that is generated from little to no effort or earned in the way of exchanging time for money over the long term. While it might take a massive amount of time and effort to establish in the beginning, passive income allows you to earn money even while you sleep with little to no daily effort required for its maintenance.

The beauty of passive income is that it is not only limited to one income bracket or portion of the population. **Anyone** can develop passive income as long as they develop the right mindset and is willing to put in the time and effort to learn and be consistent in pursuing this standard of living.

Habits and Mindset of the Financially Free

I state the habits and the mindset needed for financially free in this section because no matter how effective the strategies I will outline in the rest of this book, they will be useless unless the practitioner molds his or her mind to be consistent and persistent with them. You cannot be on and off again with the strategies that you implement to gain financial freedom.

You need to get rid of the limiting belief that what you are currently is all you can be. You need to have a mindset that promotes growth. Your mindset is your frame of mind. It is the things that you believe, your thoughts, and your opinions. Your education thus far, your upbringing, your religion, and many other things shape your mindset. Thus, your mindset determines how you perceived the outside world, yourself, and what you can achieve.

Your attitude is a manifestation of your mindset and it shows whether your mindset is limiting you or helping you to grow. A growth mindset is one that encourages making in extra time and effort to grow intelligence and experience to make a better standard of living. On the other, a fixed mindset is one where it is believed that all our qualities are fixed and born talent is the only fact determining success. This type of mindset limits a person's capacity for learning while a growth mindset is one where there is no limit to potential or success.

You need to develop a growth mindset for you to move from your current financial position to one where you are financially free. The characteristics of someone who has a growth mindset include:

- Believing that talent and intelligence can be developed through effort and learning.
- Believing that mistakes are a part of learning and that failure is an opportunity for learning and growth.

- Believing that failure is a temporary setback and not permanent feedback to ability and talent.
- Embracing challenges and change as opportunities.
- Openly receiving constructive feedback from other people for the purpose of furthering learning and development.
- Viewing constructive feedback as a valuable resource of information.
- Viewing the success of other people as a source of information and inspiration.

By opening your mind and imagining the possibilities, you can find fulfillment in not just your financial life but in your life as an entirety.

Developing a growth mindset is not something that is innately ingrained in every human being. It is something that you have to work on and the best way to do so is to develop habits that will encourage you to think differently and adaptively. Such habits include:

- **Developing your mission statement.** Success is a personal and individualized process. Therefore, if you would like to be financially free you have to know how this is meaningful to you and what financial success means to you on an individual basis.
- **Being goal-oriented.** You need to be clear on what you want out of your future and then work diligently in your effort to earn it.
- **Continually learning and seeking new experiences.** This allows you to broaden your horizons and gain you more experiences to shape your mind into one that is forward-thinking.
- **Taking action.** You will not get any results by sitting on the couch and dreaming about it. Successful people

know this and get up and do something about earning the results that they would like.
- **Being health-conscious.** The body and mind that you have now what you will have for as long as you remain on Earth. Eat right, exercise daily, keep hydrated, and keep looking to keep both your body and mind fit enough to enable you to accomplish your goals of financial freedom. Financial freedom will elude you if either of these things start to fail you.
- **Being self-disciplined.** Successful people have mastered themselves so that they can control their actions and thoughts. You cannot be dragged by your wants and desires and expect to be successful in your pursuit of financial security and independence.

Trading Options to Gain Financial Freedom

Trading options have the great potential to be a form of passive income. This is the complete opposite of active income, which is what most people engage in. Active income is one where a person invests time in exchange for money. We have discussed the pitfalls of this and seen why it should not be a person's only form of income.

Passive income allows you to still enjoy your time as you dictate while earning money. It comes to you on automatic even while you sleep. While it usually takes time, effort, and maybe monetary input at the beginning, over the long-term, if done right, you can sustain the lifestyle you want if you put forth that investment now.

Passive income:
- Gives you the platform to gain financial stability, security, and independence.

- Gives you the freedom to do whatever you wish with your time without the worry of sustaining your financial life.
- Gives you the freedom to pursue the career, hobbies, and other activities you love and enjoy rather than having to trade your time for money.
- Allows you to secure your financial future, thus getting rid of your worry, stress, and anxiety in that department.
- Gives you the flexibility to live and work from anywhere in the world, typically. The bonus of this means you get to travel if that is a pursuit you would like to take on while still earning.

Trading options can give you the benefits listed above and thus, light the way to your financial freedom.

What You Will Learn in This Book

My goal when writing this book was to show you how you can take control of your finances, pay off your debt, and live life on your own terms using one powerful strategy. Therefore, the topics that will be covered in the following pages include but are not limited to:

- What it means to trade options
- The benefits and disadvantages of trading options
- Options prices and how they are determined
- Basic options strategies for going long
- The covered call strategy
- What are strangles and straddles and how you can use them to your advantage
- Credit and debit spreads
- Iron condor
- Selling naked options
- Rolling out options

- Trader mistakes and how to avoid them
- The options trader mindset

As I mentioned above, having a growth mindset means that you openly receive information from other people to better yourself and your financial life. I am sharing my knowledge with you in this insightful guide because I have implemented these same strategies with tremendous success. It is not a perfect system but it is one that works well if done right and consistently.

Before I invite you to delve in, let me say this... To gain the most benefit from reading the information to come, you need to cultivate the growth mindset mentioned above. You have to also treat this like a business, not a side gig. This is not a hobby nor something that you are just dabbling in. Make the effort and time you invest count. Make it consistent and be persistent. Set a schedule and work on this every day. Make goals for yourself and give yourself a timeline for your accomplishments. Stay focused and committed.

The world's wealth is majorly divided into a small part of the population. Only a small percentage has financial freedom. You can put yourself and your family in that small percentile using this method for passive income. I have faith that you can do it as long as you put in that initial effort. The question is—do you believe that you can do too? Can you envision yourself as the person who has attained financial freedom in the future and is living the life you want?

Answer **YES** to both these questions and believe in that answer, I implore you!

Now, without further ado, let's jump into this invaluable guide so that you can start the future you desire today.

Chapter 1:
Options Trading Basics

There are many choices available when it comes to earning passive income and developing a strategy to gain financial freedom. Investing in real estate and trading stock are common contenders. But options trading is incomparable in terms of its affordability and accessibility.

Trading options is a powerful way of gaining financial freedom whatever it may mean to you. This is not a job that you have to show up to from 9 to 5 to benefit greatly from it. While there is some upfront human and monetary capital to be invested, once you get your feet wet, you will see the trading options are rather easy with the knowledge and experience under your belt. Next to real estate and stock trading, options trading is one of the most powerful ways to gain financial freedom passively.

What Are the Options?

An option is a financial contract called a derivative contract. It allows the owner of the contract to have the right to buy or sell the securities based on an agreed-upon price by a specified period.

That definition is rather complicated, so I will break it down into its individual components and explain each.

Option

As the name suggests, there is no obligation in this type of transaction. The trader pays for the right or the *option* to buy or sell a transaction such as security, stock, index, or ETF (exchange-traded fund) by a certain amount of time. An option is a contract.

Derivative Contract

The option *derives* its value based on the value of the underlying asset hence the term derivative contract. This contract states that the buyer agrees to purchase a specified asset within a certain amount of time at a previously agreed-upon price. Derivative contracts are often used for commodities like gold, oil, and currencies, which is often in the form of US dollars. Another type of derivative is based on the value of stocks and bonds. They can also be based on interest rates such as the yield on a specified amount of time Treasury note, as a 10-year Treasury note.

In a derivative contract, the seller does not have to own the specified asset. All they have to do is have enough money to cover the price of the asset to fulfill the contract. The seller also has the option of giving the buyer another derivative contract to offset the asset's value. These choices are often practiced because they are easier than providing the asset itself.

Securities

Securities come in several types. The great thing about securities is that they allow a person to own a specified asset without actually taking tenure of it. This makes them readily tradable because they are good indicators of the underlying value of the asset.

Common types of options securities include:

- Stock options, which use stock in a publically listed company as the asset associated with the contract.

- Index options. Similar to stocks, an index is a measure of the stocks, bonds, and other securities a company possesses.
- Currency options. Also referred to as forex options, this type of security grants the right to buy or sell a specific currency at a previously agreed-to exchange rate.
- Futures options, which gives the trader the right to assume a certain position at a future date.
- Commodity options, which is an option with an associated asset that is a physical commodity.
- Basket options. As the name suggests, this is an option made up of a group of securities.

Agreed-Upon Price

This is also known as the strike price. It does not change no matter how much time has passed and it is so named because the trader strikes when the underlying value makes him or her the desired income.

Specified Period

This is also known as the expiration date because this is the date at which the option (contract) expires. The trader can exercise the option at the strike price at any time up until the expiry date reaches. In some parts of the world such as Europe, a trader can only exercise the right to the option at the strike price exactly *on* the expiry date. We will more largely focus on the American way of trading options, which allows for exercising right on or before the expiration date.

Options vs. Stocks

Trading options and trading stocks are different because stocks and options have different characteristics. Stocks represent shares of ownership in individual companies or options. This allows the stock trader to bet in any direction that they feel the stock price is headed.

Stocks are a great investment if you are thinking of long-term yield such as for retirement and have the capital. They are very simplistic in the approach in that the trader buys the stock and wagers on the price that he or she thinks it will rise at a certain time in the future. The hope is that the price will increase in value, thus gaining the trader a substantial yield.

Stocks are also a great option for those who want to invest without having to keep a steady eye on the growth of the investment.

The risk of investing in stocks is that the price of stocks can plummet to zero at any moment. This means that the investor can lose his or her entire investment at the drop of a hat because stocks are very volatile from day to day. They are very reactive to world events such as wars, politics, scandal, epidemics, and natural disasters.

On the other hand, options are a great option for traders who would like flexibility with timing and risks. The trader is under no obligation and can see how the trade plays out over the time specified by the option contract. In that period, the price is locked which is also a great appeal.

Trading options also require a lower investment compared to stocks typically.

Another great appeal for options reading is that the specified period is typically shorter than investing in stocks. This allows for regular buying and selling as options have different expiration dates. Expiration dates can range from just a few days to several years.

The drawback that makes some people hesitate in trading options is that it is more complex than trading stocks. The trader needs to learn new jargon and vocabulary such as strike prices, calls and puts so that they can determine how to set up effective options. Not only does the trader have to learn new terms, but he or she also has to develop new skillsets and the right mindset for options trading.

Types of Trading Options

There are two major types of options:

Call Option

This type of option gives the trader the right to buy the asset on or before the expiration date. Also simply labeled a call, this type of option is traded because the price of the underlying asset is expected to rise within a certain timeframe. For the buyer of a call option, the profit lies in the price moving above the strike price. The trader can then sell the option to make a profit, which is the common call for most buyers or, choose the right to exercise the option on or before the expiration date.

The person who sells this type of option receives the premium from the trader to generate income. Therefore, the seller has a limited income while the buyer of such an option has an unlimited profit potential.

Stocks are a common asset in call option transactions. An example of a successful call options transaction is specified below using stocks as the asset.

There are 100 shares of stock up for sale. Each share is priced at $100 and therefore, a stock trader would pay $10,000 to buy these.

As an options trader, you can buy a call option that will give you the right to pay this $100 per share within a specified period of six months. The option would cost $5 per share and so, the options trader would pay a total of $500. This is a substantially lower investment than outright buying the stock. The risk is also lower than buying the stock as there is always the risk that the stock does not increase in value.

The trader had a good feeling that these stocks would increase in value though and they do by the expiration date. They are now worth $150 per share.

If the trader had bought the stock outright, he or she would make a profit of $5,000 because the stocks are now worth $15,000. As a call option, the trader would make a profit following the following formula:

(Current Price of the Stock - Strike Price) X Number of Shares = Option Worth

Using our example, this translated into:

($15,000 - $10000) x 100 = $5000

Next, to determine the profit the options trader would make, you need to remove the cost of the option. In this example, this cost was $500 and thus, the options trader makes a profit of $4,500. While this profit is slightly lower than what the stock trader made, the investment and risk were also substantially lower than outright buying the stock.

The general terms that show whether the options trader made a profit are:

- **In the money.** This means the asset price is above the call strike price as so the options trader makes a profit on the transaction.

- **Out of the money.** This means the price is below the call strike price and so the options trader makes a loss on the transaction.
- **At the money**. This means the asset price and the strike price are the same and so the options trader does not make a profit but neither does he or she make a loss on the transaction.

Put Option

This type of option gives the trader the right to sell the specified asset at the predetermined price by the expiration date. The strike price is also predetermined with this type of option. With a call option, the trader hopes that the price of the asset increases. However, with the put option, the trader hopes that the price of the asset goes down. Only if the price of the asset goes down does the trader make a profit.

Here is how this works... The trader pays for the option to sell the asset by a fixed time. If the price of the assets goes up, the trader has to sell the assets at a higher price if he or she exercises the right to the option. This is clearly a bad deal because the gap between the strike price and the selling price has narrowed.

On the other hand, exercising the right to sell the asset when it has depreciated in value widens the gap between the strike price and the sale price.

Let us take a look at how this works with an example using stock:

The trader has a feeling that 100 shares of stock will declining value soon. These 100 shares of stock are worth $100 per share now ($10,000 total). The put options trader purchase the right to sell the stock at any time within the next six months. The option costs $1.50 per share and so, the options trader pays $150.

Assuming that the options traders gut feeling pays off and the value of the stock goes down to $50 per share by the time that the expiration date arrives, this is highly profitable.

Exercising the right of the put option, the trader can sell the stock for the strike price of $100. The profit is calculated with this formula:

Asset Value - Option Cost = Profit

Therefore, using our example the profit that the trader would earn:

$10,000 - $150 = $9,850.

This is a much higher value than $5,000 that would have been earned if the trader did not exercise the put option.

The general terms that show whether the options trader made a profit are:

- **In the money.** This means the asset price is below the put strike price as so the options trader makes a profit on the transaction.
- **Out of the money.** This means the price is above the put strike price and so the options trader makes a loss on the transaction.
- **At the money**. This means the asset price and the strike price are the same and so the options trader does not make a profit but neither does he or she make a loss on the transaction.

Benefits of Trading Options

There are several advantages to trading options and they include:

- **The initial investment is lower than with trading stocks.** This means that the options trader can benefit

from playing in the same financial market as a stocks trader without paying as much upfront. This is called hedging.
- **The options trader is not required to own the asset to benefit from its value.** This means that the trader does not incur the cost associated with the asset. Costs can include transportation and storage fees if applicable.
- **There is no obligation to follow through with the transaction.** Whether the trader is exercising a call or put option, at the end of the day, the loss is limited because the trader is only obligated to pay for the contract and nothing more. Only if the trader feels it worth it does he or she take action to move forward with exercising the contract.
- **The options trader has many choices.** Trading options gives the trader great flexibility. Traders can choose to:
  - Sell the options to another investor in the case of *in the money* situations.
  - Exercise the contract and buy the asset.
  - Exercise the option and sell all or part of the asset.
  - In the case of *out of the money* situations, sell the options to another investor before the expiration date arrives.
- **The strike price freezes the price.** This allows the options trader the ability to buy or sell the asset on or before the expiration date without the worry of fluctuating prices.
- **Options can protect an asset from depreciating market prices**. This is a long term strategy that can protect assets from drops in the market prices. Exercising a call allows the trader to buy the asset at a lower price.

- **The trader can earn passive income from assets that he or she already owns.** You can sell call options on your own assets to earn income through traders paying you premiums.

Disadvantages of Trading Options

Everything has a downside and trading options are not exempted from that rule. The potential disadvantages of trading options include:

- **Option trading exposes sellers to unlimited losses.** Unlike the buyer of the option, the seller of the option faces the risk of great loss because he or she is obligated to buy or sell the asset within the time frame specified by the contract even if the price makes him or her incur a loss. The potential profit for the seller is limitless as discussed earlier and so options can be a double-edged sword because the potential losses are also limitless.
- **Options traders need to be qualified to begin trading.** This is not a business where you can just start. To trade options, an options trader needs to be approved through a broker. This approval is based on answering questions about your financial means and investment experience as well as your understanding of the risks associated with options trading. Only after the requirements have been established will the broker assign an options trader to the appropriate level based on the answers to these questions.
- **Options are typically short-term investments.** The expiration date of options is typically only a few days, weeks, or months long. This means that the option trader needs to play this financial game by having an exact strategy that he or she will implement in a near

future. There are exceptions to this rule, such as the longer-term strategy called LEAPS, which is discussed in Chapter 12.

- **There may be additional costs associated with options trading apart from the premium payments.** Often an investor in options trading needs to set up a margin account. A margin account is a line of credit that serves as collateral in the eventuality that an option incurs a loss. The settlement of this marginal account is something that your brokerage firm will guide you into the opening as each has its own minimum requirements. Luckily, the interest rates on such accounts typically stay within the single digits to low double digits. Broker commission fees are also costs that need to be considered.

Successful options traders weigh the pros and cons carefully and implement strategies to minimize the costs and potential losses while leveraging ways to make maximum profit. One of the best ways to do that is by being educated about your choices.

Tips for Getting Started With Options Trading

- **Develop a trading plan before getting started.** You need this plan to develop consistency in your actions when it comes to trading options. This will tell you how you will trade, the monies you will allocate to trading, and defines how you will track your performance. Doing this will also allow you to understand the risks involved in options so that you can plan ahead to minimize them.

- **Practicing how to earn a profit from options trading on paper first before investing actual money.** This is called paper trading and it prevents you from risking your hard-earned cash before you know what you are doing. This is done a few weeks to a few months before you do the real thing. Use spreadsheets or any other tools that make it easy for you to enter practice trades so that you can evaluate their performance over the time set for expiration. The benefits of doing this include taking away the psychological pressure of learning the mechanics without actually trading your own money.

- **Open a brokerage account.** This can be done in 2 ways—through online websites or more traditionally through a broker. This is something you need to consider carefully. Things that need to be considered include:
  - The reputation of the brokerage firm. Be sure to look out for scams, which can be especially prevalent online. Avoid websites that have bad reviews or have been reported for fraudulent activity.
  - The commissions that the brokerage firm charges. If you are lucky, you might even find a firm that does not charge commissions on options.
  - Be aware of the types of accounts that you need. They include a cash account and a margin account. A cash account is one that is loaded with cash to facilitate the buying of options. On the other hand, margin accounts allow the trader to borrow money against the value of the securities in the trader's account.
  - If you choose to trade options online, be sure that the brokerage firm accepts safe payment methods like a secure credit card payment gateway, PayPal, Payoneer, etc.
- **Ensure that you are approved to trade options.** This can be done through your brokerage firm.

- **Choose a trading style.** There are two main types of options traders. The two categories of traders are professional traders (traders that work on behalf of institutions and clients) and individual traders who trade strictly for themselves. Both of these types of traders pick from the same pool of trading styles whether or not they are trading for themselves or someone else. The different trading styles include:
  - **Day trading.** This is the method that full-time options traders use. It is more largely used by professional options traders. It involves constantly monitoring the financial markets. The name comes from the fact that the trades do not last more than a day. Profits, losses, or breakeven are realized by the end of the day and so the options are closed.
  - **Position trading.** This is a low-maintenance style that introduces low risk but requires an advanced trader's knowledge and understanding of options and the financial markets. It is mainly used by professionals.
  - **Swing trading.** This style of options trading is particularly useful for part-time trading as well as beginners who are just getting the hang of things.
  - **Market makers.** This is done in a professional capacity. Market makers are the ones who ensure that the market is liquid and has transactions to be engaged in. Without market makers, there will a low volume of options to be transacted and the trades market would be stagnant.
- **Never invest money you cannot afford or are not willing to lose.** Investing is a technique used to makes your money work for you. When it is done right, the investor will receive more money than he or she started with. However, jumping the gun can lead to losses because investing is a risk. There is no guarantee that

your money will compound itself. In fact, you may lose the entire investment. That is why you should never put up money you cannot afford to do without investing. To avoid do this, be patients, do not be greedy, and keep your costs as low as possible.
- **Never invest all your resources in one option.** This embodies the saying, "Never keep all your eggs in one basket." Remember that investing in options is a risk. Spread that risk by not limiting yourself to one option.
- **Never tie up all your capital in options trades.** This goes back to keeping your options open. Sustainable income should never come from one place. Ensure than you are doing other things to build your wealth and not solely reliant on options. Diversify your options portfolio so that all your eggs are not in the same basket.
- **Know your breakeven points.** Breakeven describes the point at which total income equals the total. We will discuss this further as we delve into options trading strategies.
- **Do your research before investing in options.** Always.
- **Anticipate losses and plan for them.**
- **If you have at least 5 losing trades back to back, stop and go back to the drawing board to discover what you are doing wrong and how you can rectify this.** Evaluate continuously your strategies to discover shortfalls.
- **Have an exit strategy for each option and know when to implement this strategy.**
- **Join online forums so that you can learn from other options traders.** This can be a valuable resource of support, information and development of technique. This is also a place you can learn from the successes and failures of other options traders so that

you do not have to repeat the failures and you can use the success stories to advance your options.

Chapter Summary

An option is a financial contract called a derivative contract. This contract allows the owner of the contract to have the right to buy or sell the securities based an agreed-upon price by a specified period. Options fall into 2 main categories. The first is called a call option. This type of option allows the trader the right to buy the asset.

The second type of option is called a put option. This type of option allows the trader the right to sell the asset.

There are several benefits to trading options versus pursuing another passive income streams such as trading stocks. These benefits include:

- The initial investment is lower than with trading stocks.
- The options trader is not required to own the asset to benefit from its value.
- There is no obligation to follow through with the transaction.
- The options trader has great flexibility.
- The strike price freezes the price at which the asset can be sold or bought.
- Options can protect an asset from depreciating market prices.
- The trader can earn passive income from assets that he or she already owns.

All things have a downside and so there are also potential disadvantages with trading options, which include:

- Options trading exposes sellers to unlimited losses.
- Options traders need to be qualified to begin trading.

- Options are typically short-term investments.
- The premium payment may not be the only cost of trading options.

Luckily, being educated about proper risk management and options trader choices can minimize these disadvantages so that the benefits far outweigh them. Having a trading plan, knowing your choices, and being aware of your breakeven point are some of the best strategies for getting started with trade options successfully.

Chapter 2:
How Options Prices are Determined

Pricing is a complex subject when it comes to options trading. Not only is the price of an option based on the value of the asset, there are other external factors that have influence.

As an options trader, you want to make sure that you maximize your efforts to make a profit. Learning how to determine the prices you should pay for options is one of the basic ways that you can ensure that your yield is as high as it can be. You do not want to be stiffed by paying higher premiums than you should.

Pricing of options is determined by several factors. Each will be stated below and discussed.

The Value of the Asset

The effect this has on options prices is straightforward. If the value of this asset goes down then exercising the option to sell becomes more valuable while the right to buy becomes less valuable.

On the other hand, if the value increases, the right to sell it becomes less valuable while the right to buy it becomes more appealing due to this increase.

The Intrinsic Value

When an options trader pays a premium, this sum represents two values. The premium is made up of the intrinsic value, which is the current value of the option and the potential increase in value that this option can obtain over time. This potential increase over time is known as the time value.

We are discussing the intrinsic value in this section. The intrinsic value is how much money the option is currently worth. It represents what the buyer would receive if he or she decided to exercise the option at the current time.

Intrinsic value is calculated by determining the difference in the current price of an asset and a strike price of the option.

For an option to have an intrinsic value of zero, the option must be out of money. Therefore, the buyer would not exercise the option because this would result in a loss. The common strategy here is allowing the option to expire so that no pay off is made. As a result, the intrinsic value results in nothing to the buyer.

For a buyer to be in the money, the intrinsic value has to be greater than the premium to increase the value of the option. This places the buyer in a position to make a profit. The intrinsic value of for in the money for call options and put options are calculated slightly differently. The formulas are as follows:

In the money call options:

Price of Asset - Strike Price = Intrinsic Value

In the money put option:

Strike Price - Price of Asset = Intrinsic Value

The Time Value

This value is the additional amount an investor is willing to contribute to the premium of an option in addition to the intrinsic value. This willingness stems from the belief that an option will increase in value before the expiration date reaches. Typically, an investor is only willing to put forth this extra amount if the option expires months away. There would be little to no change in the value of an option in a few days.

The time value is calculated by finding the difference between the intrinsic value of an option and the premium. The formula looks like this:

Option Premium - Intrinsic Value = Time Value

Therefore, the total price of an option premium follows this formula:

Intrinsic Value + Time Value = Option Premium

Both time value and intrinsic value help traders understand the value of what they are paying for if they decide to purchase an option. While the intrinsic value represents the worth of the option if the buyer were to exercise it at the current time, the time value represents the possible future value before or on the expiration date. These two values are important because they help traders understand the risk versus the reward of considering an option.

Volatility

This describes how likely a price change will occur during a specified amount of time on the financial market. If a financial market is nonvolatile then the prices change very slowly or remain unaffected over a specific amount of time. Volatile markets, on the other hand, have fast-changing prices over short periods of time.

Options traders can make use of a financial market's volatility to get a higher yield for their investment in the future. Options traders normally avoid slow-changing financial markets because these non-volatile markets often mean that no potential profit is available to the trader. Therefore, options traders thrive on volatility even though volatility increases the risk of option trading. As a result, an options trader needs to know how to read the financial market correctly to know which options are likely to yield the highest returns. This ability comes with experience, continuous learning, and keeping up to date on the happenings of the financial markets.

Many factors affect the volatility of the financial market. These factors include politics, national economics and news reports. Options traders typically use one of two options strategies to gain the best yield from volatile markets. They are called the straddle strategy and the strangle strategy. We will discuss these strategies in the upcoming chapters.

Interest Rates

Most people are familiar with the term interest rates. Interest rates apply to mortgages bank accounts and more. Interest rates as it applies to option trading is slightly different from the common variations.

The interest rate is defined as the percentage of a particular rate for the use of money lent over a period. This interest rate of an option has different effects on the call option and put option. The premiums for call options rise when interest rates rise and fall when interest rates fall. The effect is the opposite of put options. The premiums for put options fall when interest rates rise and rise when interest rates fall.

Interest rates affect the time value of options no matter what category they fall in.

You will come across the term risk-free interest rate many times in your study of options trading. This is described as the return made on an investment with no loss of capital. This is a misleading term because all investments carry some level of risk, no matter how minute. This more serves as a parameter in options pricing models such as the Black-Scholes model to determine the premium that should be paid.

Dividends

Dividends are distributions of portions of a company's profit at a specified period. This distribution must be decided and managed by the board of directors of a company. It is paid to a particular class of shareholders. Dividends can be distributed in the form of cash, shares of stock, and other types of property. Exchange-traded funds and mutual funds also pay out dividends.

As it relates to options trading, options do not actually pay dividends. However, the associated assets attached to that option can have them and thus, an options trader can receive those dividends if he or she exercises that option and takes ownership of those particular assets. While both call and put options can be affected by the presence of dividends of the associated asset, this effect on the types of options is widely varied. While the presence of dividends makes call options less expensive due to the anticipation of a drop in price, it makes put options more expensive because the price will be decreased by the amount of the dividend.

Option Pricing Models

Option pricing theory uses all of the variables mentioned above to theoretically calculate the value of an option. It is a tool that allows trainers to get an estimate of an option's fair value as they incorporate different strategies to maximize profitability. Luckily, there are models that traders can use to implement option pricing strategies to their advantage. Three commonly used pricing models for option values are:

- The Black-Scholes Model

- Binomial Option Pricing Model
- Monte-Carlo Simulations

The Black Scholes Model

Also known as the Black-Scholes-Merton (BSM) model, this pricing model won a Nobel Prize in economics because of its effectiveness. It was designed by the three economists, Fischer Black, Robert Merton and Myron Scholes in 1973. Originally used to price European options (meaning the option can only be exercised on the expiration date), this is a mathematical system that has a huge influence on modern option pricing. The pricing model helps differentiate options from gambling by determining the option premium to be paid logically. It calculates the return on the income the investor is likely to earn less the amount paid. The formulation of this amount uses the factors mentioned earlier in this chapter and others.

As this is primarily used to determine a European call option, the formula used to calculate it looks like this:

SN(d1) – Xe - rt N(d2) = Call Option Premium

The letter representations in this equation stand for:

S – Current asset price

N – A normal distribution

X – Strike price

r – risk-free interest rate

t – time of maturity

While this pricing system is great, it does have limitations. One of these limitations is that it assumes that factors like volatility and risk-free interest will remain constant, which is not the case in actuality. It also does not factor in other costs in setting up the option.

Binomial Option Pricing Model

More commonly used to develop pricing for American options, this pricing system was developed in 1979. Even as popular as the Black Scholes Model is, this model is even more frequently used in practice because it is more intuitive. This pricing system allows the assumption that there are two possible outcomes—one where the outcome moves up and one where the outcome moves down.

This system differs from the Black Scholes Model that it allows calculations for multiple periods whereas the Black Scholes Model does not. This advantage gives a multi-period view, which is very advantageous to options traders.

This model makes use of binomial trees to figure out options pricing. These are diagrams with a main formula branching off into two different directions. This branching is what gives the multi-period view that this pricing system is famous for.

For this pricing system to work, the following assumptions are made:

- There are 2 possible prices for the associated asset, hence the name of the pricing system. Bi means 2.
- The 2 possibilities involve the price of the asset moving up or down.
- There are no dividends being paid on the asset.
- The rate of interest does not change through the life of the option
- There are no risks attached to the transaction.
- There are no other costs associated with the option.

Clearly, just like with the Black Scholes Model, there is some limitation with those assumptions. Still, the pricing system is highly valuable in the valuing of American options due to the fact that such options can be exercised any time until the expiration date.

Monte Carlo Simulations

Used in multiple fields across the board like science, engineering, and finance, this model allows the options trader to consider multiple outcomes due to the involvement of random factors. It allows for the consideration of risk and unpredictability, unlike the first two pricing models. This is why it is also sometimes called multiple probability simulation.

A Final Word on Pricing

The reason I went into such depth on pricing options is because I want you to realize that everything related to options requires careful consideration right down to the premiums paid. This needs to be a fair trade for all the parties involved and premium pricing needs to reflect that fairness. When considering the options premium, remember to search deeper than the surface level to ensure that fairness and to ensure that you are gaining the profit that you need out of the transaction.

Chapter Summary

There are 6 factors that determine the price of options. They are:

- The value of the asset
- The intrinsic value, which is the determination of the difference an asset current price and an option strike price.
- The time value, which is the difference between the intrinsic value of an option and the premium.

- Volatility, which is how likely a price change will occur during a specified amount of time on the financial market.
- Interest rates, which are the percentage of a particular rate for the use of money lent over a period.
- Dividends, which are distributions of portions of a company's profit at a specified period.

All of these factors help make up the formal pricing models used to determine option premiums. 3 common pricing models are:

- The Black-Scholes Model
- Binomial Option Pricing Model
- Monte-Carlo Simulations

Chapter 3:
Basic Options Strategies Going Long

Going Long vs. Going Short

As an options trader, you will often hear the terms going long or having a long position and going short or taking a short position. The positions are opposites. Both terms refer to what the investor owns and what he or she needs to own to be effective at options trading.

Having a short position means that the investor does not own the assets being associated with the option. For example, there may be an option for the sale of 100 shares but the investor doing the selling does not own the shares.

On the other hand, having a long position means that the investor owns the asset associated with the option. For example: an investor who bought and adds 100 shares to his or her portfolio has a long position. This investor likely bought this asset, which can be stock, commodity, or currency with the expectation that the value will rise. This is known as having a bullish view. A bullish view describes the characteristic of an investor pursuing an asset with the feeling that it will appreciate because they wish to limit any potential losses.

There is another view that can affect if an options trader decides to hold a long position. The trader may try to make a profit but the fall of an asset's value. This can be advantageous because the trader can obtain an option to sell that asset at a price that is advantageous to him or her.

As it relates to options trading, the long position refers to whether or not the trader will hold a long call or long put option. This is dependent on the associated asset attached to that contract. Holding a long call option means that the trader expects that the price of the asset will go up so that he or she can benefit in that regard. The option allows the trader to buy that asset at the strike price so that the upward trend is fulfilled.

With a long put option, the trader expects the asset to depreciate so that he or she can purchase the right to sell that asset at a predetermined price.

In both cases, the long position does not in any way refer to the period. The focus is entirely on the associated asset and who owns it. The person who owns the asset is called the long position holder.

One of the biggest benefits of a long position is an option of this nature locks in the strike prices. Losses are limited because the trader can base his or her bets on historic market performance.

Unfortunately, there are disadvantages to going long. Firstly, the financial market may become volatile and cause abrupt price changes. This may not be for the benefit of the options trader. Secondly, the option may reach its expiration date before the advantage the options trader was hoping to achieve is realized.

Simple Going Long Strategies

Of course, there are very complicated going long strategies that can be employed but as a beginner, it is best to start simply and get a lay of the land. This is why I have stuck to the basics in this chapter and will continue in the same way with the two most common and simple going long strategies.

Long Call

As mentioned earlier, this strategy is considered by options traders who want to make a profit from an asset that increases in the price above the strike price. This is often considered so that the trader does not have to buy the asset outright so that he or she can potentially profit without having to take on the major risk of owning that asset.

This type of option can also afford the trader access to assets he or she cannot afford to purchase at that time. This is a common practice in accessing stock. Having the option to purchase is less expensive than purchasing the stock outright.

Here is a summary of how a long call works:

Outlook: Bullish

Risk: The premium paid

Potential profit: Unlimited. It increases as the price of the asset increases.

Break-even price: The sum of the strike price and premium paid **(strike price + premium paid)**

An example of a successful long call is as follows:

An options trader buys 100 shares of stock that he believes will increase in value within the next few months. Each share costs $20. He believes the shares will go up by at least $10. Therefore, he buys the option at a strike price of $20 plus a cost of $2 for each stock, which totals $22 per stock.

As long as the stock goes above $22, this long call option is profitable to the trader. For every dollar the stock goes higher, the trader will profit $100. As the stock price increases, so does the option value. Therefore, the trader can sell the option to lock in his profit.

The best thing about such an option is that the asset can infinitely increase in value which can lead to massive profits. This is why long calls are a popular way to bet on rising stock prices.

In this case, this is also a risk that the trader will lose his or her investment in the cost of the premium and associated fees. The asset may not become advantageous before the expiration date arrives and thus, the option becomes worthless to the trader.

Long Put

This type of option gives the trader the right to sell the associated asset at the strike price on or before the expiration date. The options trader makes a profit from the asset decreasing to a price below the strike price. As you can see, this is very similar to the long call and only differs in the fact that the trader is betting on the fact that the value of the asset will fall below the strike price on or before the expiration date.

Long puts are a great way of protecting the value of assets that you already own.

Here is a summary of how a long call works:

Outlook: Bearish (Falling prices)

Risk: The premium paid

Potential profit: Unlimited. It increases as the price of the asset decreases.

Break-even price: The difference between the strike price and premium paid **(strike price - premium paid)**

An example of a successful long put is as follows:

A company is trading stock at $50 per share. An options trader feels that the price of this will fall to at least $30 per share within the coming months and so, seeks a put option with a strike price of $50 that had an expiration date of 2 months. He buys 100 shares and pays $150 to purchase each $50 share. The option is priced at $5 per share and so, the trader pays $500.

The trader was right and the price of the stock depreciates to $25 per share before the expiration date. With the current stock price, the trader with the put option will be in the money because the intrinsic value of the stock has risen. Let's say that this value is now $1500. The trader can sell the stock for that price. The trader will make a profit of $1000 after removing his investment of $500.

The great advantage in this scenario is similar to the advantage in the long call, hence why this too is a popular way of betting on declining stock values. As a result, a long put is a great option if the trader expects the price of the asset to fall significantly before the expiration date arrives. If the price falls only a little or not at all, the trader may be in the money only slightly, which is not profitable, or worse, it may not even return the premium the trader spent.

Chapter Summary

The long position in options trading refers to the fact that the investor owns the asset associated with the option. This is comparable to the short position, where the investor does not own the asset being associated with the option.

As it relates to options trading, the long position refers to whether or not the trader will hold a long call or long put option. This is dependent on the associated asset attached to that contract. Holding a long call option means that the trader expects that the price of the asset will go up so that he or she can benefit in that regard. The option allows the trader to buy that asset at the strike price if that upward trend is fulfilled.

With a long put option, the trader expects the asset to depreciate so that he or she can purchase the right to sell that asset at a predetermined price.

While this can be disadvantageous in that there is no guarantee the advantage will be realized by the expiration date and this is a risky move in the short-term, the benefits include:

- Having a locked strike price even if the profits grow beyond expectations.
- The losses are limited.
- This move can rely on historical data to maximize profit.

Using both the long call and long put strategies can be highly advantageous to options traders.

Chapter 4:
Covered Call Strategy (or Protected Puts)

What Is a Covered Call?

Also known as a buy-write, this describes the act of selling the right to purchase a specified asset that you own at a specified price within a specified amount of time, which is usually less than 12 months. It is a two-part strategy whereby someone first purchases stock then sells it on the share by share prices.

The beauty of this type of option is off the bat, the seller benefits by receiving a premium payment from the options holder. Risk is mitigated because the seller already owns the stock. Therefore, your costs are covered if the stock price rises above the strike price. If the trader chooses to exercise the right to purchase on or before the expiration date, you simply deliver as agreed and rip any additional benefits.

Stock is the most common asset used in this type of option.

If you choose to consider covered calls, you need to be willing to own the stock at your price it is even if the price depreciates. Remember that there is no guarantee that you will earn greatly on the stock that you have purchased due to the volatility of financial markets. Therefore, you need to be diligent in your focus on seeking good quality stocks that you are willing to own. You need to be able to still potentially benefit from that ownership if there are down periods in the market.

As the seller of a covered call option, you need to be also willing to part with that stock if the price rises. You cannot change your mind if the price of the stock goes up if you have already entered into an option with a willing buyer. You must exercise that delivery if the trader chooses to exercise that option.

The maximum potential profit of covered calls is achieved if the stock price is met at or above the strike price of that call at or by the expiration date. The formula for this is as follows:

Sum of the Call Premium + (Strike Price - Stock Price) = Maximum Potential Profit

The seller also needs to consider the break-even point at the expiration date. The formula for this is as follows:

Purchase Price of the Stock - The Call Premium = Break-Even Analysis

The seller also needs to determine the maximum risk potential. This is equal to the purchasing price of the stock at the break-even point.

The seller also needs to be satisfied with the static rate of return and the if-called rate of return on the stocks. The static return is the approximate annual net profit of a covered call, assuming that the stock price does not change until the expiration date and until the option expires. To calculate this value, the seller needs to know:

- The purchase price of the particular stock
- The strike price of the option
- The price of the call
- The number of days until option expires
- If there are any dividends and the amount of these dividends

Calculating these factors leads to a percentile figure being determined. The formula for calculating this is:

(Call + Dividend) / Stock Price × Time Factor = Static Rate of Return

The if-called return is an approximate annual net profit on a covered call with the assumption that the stock price is above the strike price by or on the expiration of the option and the stock is sold at expiration. To calculate this figure, which is also a percentage, the same factors need to be determined. The formula for calculating this is:

(Call + Dividend) + (Strike − Stock Price) / Stock Price × Time Factor = If-Called Rate of Return

Benefits of Covered Call Options

The first benefit of covered call options is the seller receives a premium payment, which can be kept as income whether or not the trader chooses to exercise the right to the option. This can be set up as a regular cash flow by serious investors in markets that are relatively neutral or bullish. The investor can set up a program for selling covered calls regularly. This can potentially set up a monthly or quarterly income stream.

The second benefit of covered calls is that they can help investors target a selling price for a particular stock that is above the current price. Lastly, covered calls have the additional benefit of limiting risks as the asset provides protection to the seller.

The Risks Associated with Covered Call Options

The first major risk associated with covered calls is that the seller can lose money if the stock price depreciates below the break-even point. This is a risk that anyone who owns stock takes on.

The second risk is not being able to anticipate a huge price rise in the price of the stock. Stocks have unlimited profit potential but if the holder of the options for that stock chooses to exercise his or her right then the seller has to hand it over to this person. This can lead to a great missed opportunity as the seller now has to hand over a tremendous asset in the transaction.

How to Create a Covered Call Option

The first step in creating a covered call is purchasing the stock. This is done by purchasing it in lots of 100 shares. Doing this allows you to sell an option for every 100 shares of stocks. The great thing about buying stock in this way is that you do not have to option all of them. For example, let's say that you bought 1000 shares of stock. You can sell 5 contracts, leveraging 500 shares, and earning 5 premium payments. You will hold onto 500 shares of stock even if the holders of the options of those 5 contracts exercise their right.

The last step is waiting for the covered call to be exercised or for it to expire. If the covered calls are not exercised, then you still get to keep the premium. There is always the option to buy the option back before the expiration date arrives but sellers hardly ever do this. Remember that you have to be willing to part with the stock once you option it.

How the Covered Call Works

Covered calls work in one of three ways.

The Stock Price Goes Down

In this case, the covered call will be worthless on expiration. The bad news is that the stock price goes down but the good news is that the seller gets to keep the premium and so still earned from the transaction. The decrease in the price of the stock is simply the nature of owning stocks. You should have accounted for this before you made the purchase. Remember that you need to be willing to own that stock no matter what, so choose wisely. Note though that the profit from selling the call can help offset this decrease in the price of the stock.

The stock price may fall before the expiration date. This is not caused for fret because you are not indefinitely locked in this position. Even though the stock price has gone down and the call value went down as well, this is an opportunity to buy the call back for less money than you sold it for.

The Stock Price Does Not Change or Goes Up Slightly

This is not a losing scenario. While the covered call will expire as worthless, the seller still keeps the premium for the option. If you see a slight rise in the price of the stock, while the holder of the option is unlikely to exercise the right to gain that, the seller benefits from it nonetheless even if the rise is marginal.

The Stock Goes Above the Strike Price

If the stock goes up above the strike price by the expiration date, the holder of the option will exercise the right and the seller needs to sell the 100 shares of stock. It is a hard pill to swallow if the price of the stock skyrockets even if you already reconciled a willingness to part with the stock before but comfort yourself with the fact that you gain maximum profit from the transaction.

Chapter Summary

A covered call is a tactic of a seller selling the right to purchase a specified asset that he or she owns at a specified price within a specified amount of time, which is usually less than 12 months. The main goal of creating such a covered call is to collect premium payments as a source of income against stock that is already owned.

To do this effectively, the seller must:

- Be willing to own the stock at the price it is even if the price depreciates.
- Be willing to part with that stock if the price rises.
- Be satisfied with the static rate of return and if-called rate of return on the stocks.

A covered call is created by first buying stocks in lots of 100 shares. Next, the seller creates covered calls with the 100 shares decided upon. Lastly, all the seller has to do is wait to see if the contract holder will exercise the option or allow it to expire.

The cover call will play out in one of 3 ways. Either:

- The stock price goes down. While the call will be worthless, the seller gets to keep the premium.
- The stock does not change or goes up slightly. While the call will be worthless, the seller gets to keep the premium.
- The stock goes above the strike price. The holder will exercise the right and the seller needs to sell thereby earning a maximum profit on the transaction.

The benefits of the covered call include:

- Earning a premium payment for the covered call in the form of premium payment.
- Helping investors target a selling price for a particular stock that is above the current price.
- Limiting risks as the price of the stock provides protection to the seller.

There are also risks associated with the covered call and they are:

- The seller can lose money if the stock price depreciates below the break-even point. However, this is a risk that any stock owner takes on.
- Not being able to anticipate a huge price rise in the price of the stock, which can result in an opportunity cost.

Chapter 5:
Strangles and Straddles

Both strangles and straddles are options strategies that allow the investor to benefit whether the stock price goes up or down. They carry similarities such as buying an equal number of call options (options that give the trader the right to buy the stock) and put options (options that give the trader the right to sell the stock), the same asset and they both have the same expiration date.

The difference lies in the number of strike prices. The strangle has 2 separate strike prices while the straddle has 1 common strike price.

These two strategies are called volatile strategies because unlike many strategies that bet on if options are bullish or bearish, these strategies bet on the volatility of the financial market.

Types of Volatility

There are five different types of volatility as it relates to financial markets. The first one that we will discuss is known as price volatility. Price volatility describes how the prices of assets move up or down. This type of volatility is affected by the supply and demand of that asset. There are external factors that affect supply and demand. Prices may rise up and down due to the season. For example, prices may fluctuate due to whether or not it is summer or winter in the tourism industry. This factor fluctuates because of demand. Weather is another factor that can affect price volatility. For example, financial markets in the agricultural sector fluctuate due to the supply of certain crops at certain times of the year in certain regions. Emotions are also something that causes price volatility. For example, because of emotional attachment, gas prices continue to be high because there is a huge demand.

Stocks are also highly volatile. The characteristic is called stock volatility. This unpredictable nature is what makes stock a risky investment. Even though the returns on investing in stock can be quite high, the losses can be disastrous as well. This is why there is a science to picking stocks that are likely to be profitable. Investors use the measurement known as a beta to predict stock's volatility.

The financial market has a beta measure of 1.0. Individual stocks are ranked according to how they deviate away from the market. Therefore, stocks that increase more than the market over time have a beta that is greater than 1.0 while stocks that go below the market have a beta that is less than 1.0.

Stocks that have a beta of greater than 1.0 are risky to invest in but also have a higher potential for returns. Stocks that have a beta that is below 1.0 are less risky to invest in but also typically have lower returns. Beta is calculated with the following formula:

Variance / Covariance = Beta

Covariance is a measure of a stock's sensitivity relative to that of the financial market while variance is a measure of how the market moves relative to its mean.

Another type of volatility is called historical volatility. This is a measure of how a stock has performed over the last 12 months. If a stock's prices varied wildly over that period, it is very volatile and therefore, risky to invest in. If a stock was less volatile over that period, it becomes more attractive to invest in. An investor may, however, choose to hold onto the stock for a longer period so that greater returns are achieved. To gain maximum profitability, the trader will study the market to see when is the best time to sell the stock at the highest value. This technique is called timing the market and as such, this technique does not work with volatile stocks because they are unpredictable.

Implied volatility is a measure of how a stock will perform in the future. This is an opinion as there is no guarantee of what will happen in the future. Generating this opinion depends on certain factors that can be accounted for in the present. These factors include:

- The price of the stock
- The market price of the option
- The expiry date of the option
- The interest rate
- The strike price
- Dividends

While implied volatility in no way evaluates stock, it does evaluate how options should be prepared for selling and buying. It helps develop a fair price for the option so that it is profitable even if the price of the stock goes down. An option's price sensitivity in relation to implied volatility is known as 'vega.' This figure represents the amount that an option price will change in reaction to a 1% change in the implied volatility of the stock.

Vega is one of the Greeks. These are a collection of degrees that provide a measure of an option's sensitivity in relation to other factors. Other measures include delta, gamma, and theta. Delta describes the option's sensitivity in relation to the-price of the stock. Theta describes an option's sensitivity in relation to how time affects the premium of an option. Gamma is a reflection of the rate of change of the delta.

Other Greeks include:
- Lambda, which describes an option's sensitivity in relation to the associated asset's value.
- Rho, which describes an option's sensitivity to the interest rate.

The last type of volatility is known as market volatility and it describes the rate at which prices change on any financial market.

All of these types of volatility affect how an options trader will utilize strangles and straddles strategies.

We will now look at the benefits and risks of each of these strategies below.

The Strangle Strategy

This strategy is employed when the trader strongly believes that the stock price will move either up or down but still wants to be protected in case he or she is wrong. There are both long and short strangles.

The Short Strangle

Also called a sell strangle, this is a neutral options trading strategy. The trader sells:

- 1 out of the money put
- 1 out of the money call

Both of these will have the same associated stock and the same expiration date. This is a tactic employed when the trader thinks that the stock will be relatively stable on the market in the short term. Profit is gained when the stock prices on the expiration date are between the strike prices of the options. This profit is limited. The formula for this profit is calculated like this:

Premium Received - Commissions Paid = Profit

Unfortunately, the risk of this type of option is unlimited. Loss is experienced if the price of the stock goes up or down sharply by the expiration date.

With a call option, this is calculated this way:

Price of Stock - Strike Price of Short Call - Premium Received = Loss

The loss with the put option is calculated with this formula:

Strike Price of Short Put - Price of Stock - Net Premium Received + Commissions Paid = Loss

There are 2 breakeven points with such a transaction. Calculated on the short call, the formula is this:

Strike Price of Short Call + Premium Received = Breakeven

The formula for the short put breakeven point looks like this:

Strike Price of Short Put - Premium Received = Breakeven

The Long Strangle

This is also called the buy strangle and it is based in a neutral position in the options trading. The trader buys:

- 1 out of the money put
- 1 out of the money call

Both of these will have the same associated stock and the same expiration date.

This is a strategy that is used when a trader believes that there will be great volatility in the market. The beauty of this strategy is that it minimizes the risk of loss and introduces the potential for unlimited profit. This profit is gain when the price of the stock takes a sharp move up or down. The formula for the call option is:

Price of stock - Strike Price of Long Call - Premium Paid = Profit

The formula for the put option is:

Strike Price of Long Put - Price of Stock - Premium Paid = Profit

The risk of this type of strategy is that the stock prices are trading between the strike prices of the options bought on the expiration date. Both options will become worthless.

Net loss is calculated with this formula:

Premium Paid + Commissions Paid = Loss

The trader can breakeven at 2 points with this strategy. The formula for breakeven on the call option is:

Strike Price of Long Call + Premium Paid = Breakeven

The formula for breakeven on the put option is:

Strike Price of Long Put - Premium Paid = Breakeven

The Straddle Strategy

With this options trading strategy, the trader protects himself regardless of if the price of the stock moves up or down. Think of it as someone straddling a fence. This person can jump to either side of the fence to ensure the situation benefits him or her. There are both long and short straddles.

The Short Straddle

This is also called a sell straddle as well as a naked straddle sale. This neutral options strategy work by the trader selling:

- 1 at the money call
- 1 at the money put

The options have the same associated stock, strike price, and expiration date.

These types of transactions have a limited profit just like short strangle. The profit is achieved when the stock price trades at the strike price of the options on the expiration date. The formula for calculating this is:

Net Premium Received - Commissions Paid = Profit

The risk is unlimited and is incurred when the stock prices moves up or down by the expiration date. On the call option, the formula for calculating this is:

Price of Underlying - Strike Price of Short Call - Net Premium Received = Loss

For calculating the loss on the put option, this formula is used:

Strike Price of Short Put - Price of Stock - Net Premium Received + Commissions Paid = Loss

This strategy also has 2 breakeven points. Calculating the breakeven on the call looks like this:

Strike Price of Short Call + Premium Received = Breakeven

Calculating the breakeven on the put looks like this:

Strike Price of Short Put - Premium Received = Breakeven

The Long Straddle

Also known as the buy straddle, this strategy is a neutral one whereby the trader buys:

- 1 at the money call
- 1 at the money put

This strategy ensures that both options have the same associated stock, strike price, and expiration date.

The profits associated with this strategy are unlimited. Because the trader has long positions on both the call and put options, profits grow when the stock prices move up or down strong enough. Profit is calculated with the following formulas:

Price of Stock - Strike Price of Long Call - Net Premium Paid = Profit

Strike Price of Long Put - Price of Stock - Net Premium Paid = Profit

Another benefit of using this strategy is the risks are limited as the loss is incurred when the stock price trades at the strike price on the expiration date. Loss is calculated with this formula:

Premium Paid + Commissions Paid = Loss

Just like with all of the strategies mentioned above, breakeven for long straddle is calculated at 2 points. The formulas for calculating this as follows:

Strike Price of Long Call + Net Premium Paid = Breakeven

Strike Price of Long Put - Net Premium Paid = Breakeven

Chapter Summary

Both strangles and straddles are neutral options strategies that allow the investor to benefit whether the stock price goes up or down. They have similar characteristics, which are an equal number of call options and put options, the same asset and they both have the same expiration date. They only differ in the number of strike prices called on the options.

The strangle strategy is employed when the trader strongly believes that the stock price will move either up or down but still wants to be protected in case he or she is wrong.

Using the straddle strategy, the trader protects himself or herself regardless of if the price of the stock moves up or down. Both strategies have a long and short option. They are both affected by the volatility of the financial market.

Chapter 6:
Credit and Debit Spreads

Credit Spreads vs. Debit Spreads

The use of spreads is another tactical approach to options trading. The spread is described as the purchase and sale of two different options with the same associate asset attached.

Credit spreads describe the selling of a high-premium option while purchasing a low-premium option in the same class (calls or puts). This results in a credit to the investor's account. Both of these options have the same expiration date but different strike prices. The aim here is to make a profit when the spread between the two options becomes narrowed.

On the other hand, a debit spread is one where the trader buys a high-premium option and sells a low-premium option with the same associated asset attached to both options. Just like with a credit spread, both options have the same expiration date but different strike prices. The trader makes a profit when the spread between the two options widens. This results in a debit to the trader's account.

Credit Spreads

How Credit Spreads Work

A credit spread is advantageous because the seller collects more in premium than what is paid out in the options. For example, if the trader sells an option for $1000 and buys another option at a lower strike price of $75 then they will have a net result of $25. We refer to this as a credit because they is collecting more than they is paying out.

There are several types of credit spreads but we will focus on 2 in this section—the put credit spread and the call credit spread. The put credit spread has a bullish outlook and relies on time decay. The profit comes when the stock prices increase. Profit for 100 shares of stock is calculated with this formula:

Credit Received x 100 = Profit

The loss for 100 shares of stock is calculated with this formula:

(Width of the two Strike Prices - Credit Received) x 100 = Loss

Breakeven is calculated with this formula:

Short Put Strike Price - Credit Received = Breakeven

The call credit spread is approached with bearish outlook and it too relies on time decay. Profits are realized when stock prices decrease. Profit for 100 shares of stock is calculated with this formula:

Credit Received x 100 = Profit

The loss for 100 shares of stock is calculated with this formula:

(Width of the two Strike Prices - Credit Received) x 100 = Loss

Breakeven is calculated with this formula:

Short Call Strike Price - Credit Received = Breakeven

Types of Credit Spreads

- **Bull Put Spread:** This is a great option strategy for beginners to implement. It is a bearish technique that relies on the price of the

associated asset going down significantly enough but not by a huge jump. Two transactions are required with an upfront cost. The trader:
- ✓ Buys 1 out of the money put
- ✓ Sells 1 on the money put

They are implemented by buying a lower-premium out of the money put option while simultaneously selling one in the money put option that is of a higher premium.

Profit is achieved when the price of the associated asset is equal to the credit received from the options. The formula for this is:

Premium Received - Commissions Paid = Profit

Loss occurs when the stock prices go below the strike price on or before the expiration date. This is calculated with this formula:

Strike Price of Short Put - Strike Price of Long Put Net Premium + Commissions Paid = Loss

Breakeven is calculated like this:

Strike Price of Short Put - Net Premium Received = Breakeven

- **Bear Call Spread:** This type of option works similarly to the one stated above and profit is reliant on the prices of the associated asset falling moderately. The trader:
  - ✓ Buys 1 out of the money call
  - ✓ Sells 1 in the money call

Profit is calculated with this formula:

Premium Received - Commissions Paid = Profit

Loss occurs when the stock prices go above the strike price on or before the expiration date. This is calculated with this formula:

Strike Price of Long Call - Strike Price of Short Call - Net Premium Received + Commissions Paid = Loss

Breakeven is calculated like this:

Strike Price of Short Call + Net Premium Received = Breakeven

This bearish strategy is slightly more complicated and is not typically recommended for novice options traders.

- **Short Butterfly Spread:** This is a volatility-based strategy that is typically practiced by medium to advanced options traders. This applies to both call and put options of this type. Three transactions are involved. They are:
    - ✓ Buying 1 in the money call/put
    - ✓ Selling 1 out of the money call/put
    - ✓ Buying 1 as the money call/put

This is not an options trading strategy that a trader should jump into lightly. This requires careful thought and consideration. Thus, this is a strategy that is best employed by intermediate and advanced options traders. However, when done right, this strategy offers benefits like increased flexibility and the ability to profit no matter which direction the price of the asset goes. Both the profit and loss of this type of strategy are limited. This limitation is great for managing risks.

- **Iron Butterfly Spread:** This is a neutral strategy that entails 4 transactions. The trader:
    - ✓ Buys 1 out of the money call

- ✓ Sells 1 at the money call
- ✓ Buys 1 out of the money put
- ✓ Sells 1 at the money put

The two calls and puts of this options strategy are equal and the associated asset and expiration date of all of these components are the same. Due to the complexity of this strategy, it is not suitable for beginners. The higher commissions also make it less appealing to most traders. However, the benefits include a higher potential profit. This strategy is useful for making a huge payout. Thus, on such a sizable contract, the commissions' increase may be worth pursuing this strategy.

Pros and Cons of Credits Spreads

One of the biggest advantages of using credit spreads is that they drastically lower the risk to the trader if the stock price moves against the trader. Next, the seller receives cash upfront in the form of premium payment. Losses are limited because the trader stands to benefit no matter what direction the price of the associated asset moves.

The biggest disadvantage of this type of option strategy is that it requires a trader to use a margin account. This is not something a trader might necessarily want to do. Also, another disadvantage is even though the losses are limited so are the profits.

Debit Spreads

How Debit Spreads Work

Unlike a credit spread where the seller receives cash into his or her account, debit spreads instead carry an upfront cost. The premium is paid from the investor's account when the position is opened, and this is referred to as a debit. This type of strategy is mostly used to offset the costs associated with having long option positions. This results because the premium received from long components is more than the premium received from short components. As a result of this, the net debt is the highest possible value for loss in this type of option strategy. Losses are thus limited.

Despite this upfront cost, debit spreads are generally considered safer to create and less complicated than credit spreads. Debit spreads are therefore more commonly used by beginners compared to credit spreads.

Just like the credit spreads, there are at least two options involved in the transaction. The trader pays for a higher premium option while selling a lower-premium option. However, just like with credit spreads the number of transactions executed in this strategy can exceed 2.

Just like with credit spreads, there are call and put versions. The basic call version is set up like this—the investor:

- Buys 1 call
- Sells 1 call (this is the higher strike)

Profit is calculated with this formula:

Width of the two Strike Prices – Premium – Commissions = Profit

Loss is calculated with this formula:

Premium Paid + Commissions = Loss

With the put option, the set up looks like this:

- Sell 1 put
- Buy 1 put (this is the higher strike)

Profit is calculated with this formula:

Width of the two Strike Prices − Premium − Commissions = Profit

Loss is calculated with this formula:

Premium Paid + Commissions = Loss

All of these equations will be x100 to prepare a contract with 100 shares as the associated asset.

Types of Debit Spreads

- **Bull Call Spread:** This is a relatively simple strategy to implement as it only requires 2 transactions. The trader:
  - ✓ Buys 1 at the money call
  - ✓ Sells 1 out of money call

This is a bullish strategy that is implemented when the trader believes that the price of the associated asset will rise moderately.

Profit is achieved when the price of the associated asset is equal to the strike prices of the short call. The formula for this is:

Strike Price of Short Call - Strike Price of Long = Profit

Loss occurs when the stock price goes below the strike price on or before the expiration date. This is calculated with this formula:

Net Premium Paid + Commissions Paid = Loss

Breakeven is calculated like this:

Strike Price of Long Call + Net Premium Paid = Breakeven

- **Bear Put Spread:** This is a bearish strategy that is used when a trader believes that the price of the associated asset will go down by a moderate amount. It only requires 2 transactions and is, therefore, suitable for beginners. The trader:
    - ✓ Buys 1 at the money put
    - ✓ Sells 1 on the money put

This is a straightforward strategy that has limited losses and profits with comparatively low upfront costs.

Profit is achieved when the price of the associated asset is equal to the strike prices of the short call. The formula for this is:

Width of the two Strike Prices - Net Premium Paid - Commissions Paid = Profit

Loss occurs when the stock price goes above the strike price on or before the expiration date. This is calculated with this formula:

Net Premium Paid + Commissions Paid = Loss

Breakeven is calculated like this:

Strike Price of Long Put + Net Premium Paid = Breakeven

- **Reverse Iron Butterfly:** This is a volatile strategy that is used when a trader believes that the price of the associated asset will move sharply at price but is not sure in which direction. Thus, this strategy is created to gain a profit no matter the direction. It requires 4 transactions and they are:
    - ✓ Sell 1 out of money put
    - ✓ Buy 1 at the money put

- ✓ Buy 1 at the money call
- ✓ Sell 1 out of money call

The profit gained in this type of strategy is limited and is achieved when the associated asset price drops below the strike price. The formula for this is:

Width of the two Strike Prices - Net Premium Paid - Commissions Paid = Profit

Loss occurs when the stock price is the same as the strike price on the expiration date. This is calculated with this formula:

Net Premium Paid + Commissions Paid = Loss

The 2 breakeven points for this strategy are calculated like this:

Strike Price of Long Call + Net Premium Paid = Breakeven

Strike Price of Long Put + Net Premium Paid = Breakeven

- **Butterfly Spread:** This is a neutral strategy that involves 3 transactions. The trader:
    - ✓ Buys 1 in the money call
    - ✓ Sells 2 at the money calls
    - ✓ Buys 1 on the money call

The profit gained in this type of strategy is limited and is achieved when the associated asset price remains unchanged on the expiration date. The formula for this is:

Width of the two Strike Prices - Net Premium Paid - Commissions Paid = Profit

Loss is also limited. It occurs when the stock price is the same as the strike price on the expiration date. This is calculated with this formula:

Net Premium Paid + Commissions Paid = Loss

The 2 breakeven points for this strategy are calculated like this:

Strike Price of Higher Strike Long Call - Net Premium Paid = Breakeven

Strike Price of Lower Strike Long Call + Net Premium Paid = Breakeven

This is not a strategy that is recommended for beginners but it can indeed bring in a high return on investment. Unfortunately, because of the higher number of transactions, the commissions paid on this strategy can be high.

Pros and Cons of Debit Spreads

The benefits of debits spreads include:

- They aid in trade planning because they help the trader determined potential maximum profits and losses in advance.
- Losses are limited due to how these types of strategies are implemented.
- Margin accounts are not required for this type of option strategy and can be used by traders who cannot use them.
- They offer greater profit margins.

There are also disadvantages to these types of options strategies. The biggest is that the profit margin is limited just as the losses are limited.

Legging Spreads

Every option trader runs into the question of whether or not he or she should leg an option. This section is dedicated to breaking down the process and giving you legit reasons why you can consider legging as a technique to leverage opportunities as well as minimize the risks associated with the technique. The legging is a technique that is associated with having multiple transactions associated with one option. Of course, this can become quite complicated but the basic concept remains the same always.

What is Legging?

Spreads by their nature of having more than one transaction with the same associated asset make them the perfect opportunity to engage in a legging. Every spread has at least two legs—the buying of one option and the selling of another. Normally these two transactions occur at the same time but there are instances where the trader separates the transactions. This process of separating the transactions is called legging.

Legging comes from the term leg, which describes a singular component on an options trading strategy. When several components are put together, it becomes legging. Legging does not only have to consist of two transactions. It can become a lot more complicated with many more transactions.

Benefits of Legging

The legging is widely used by experienced options traders and they find it beneficial for several reasons, including:

- It might result in losses if the transactions are done at the same time and so legging allows the components to be done individually.

- It might be possible to make a bigger profit by legging into or out of a certain position.
- The broker may not be in a position to carry out each transaction at the same time.
- The market climate may have changed and made it necessary to leg into another position for profitability's sake.
- Legging may be needed to lock in a profit or ensure losses stay to a minimum.

Luckily, using online brokerage firms has greatly reduced the likelihood of the third case being the scenario that pushes an options trader to use the legging technique but it still exists. Be careful with transacting legs with your brokerage firm as while the strategy might be profitable by its self, the fees and commissions from doing multiple transactions at the same time can stack up quickly and cut on the potential profits. Still, many online brokers allow for multiple transactions without making a fuss. It is typically a built-in feature because of its potential to greatly increase profitability by combining several transactions to build one powerful position.

How to Use Legging

Implementing legging is a matter of priority. You need to know which leg you will execute first and the order the subsequent legs will fall. In slow-moving markets, the order may not be as important to perfect but in fast-moving markets where prices fall and rise in rapid succession, this order is paramount. Understanding the market is what will lead to correctly determining this order. This is why options traders need to be on the ball to make legging work.

After studying the market for the right conditions for the strategies, the trader then needs to develop a plan to execute each leg.

The Risks of Legging

The legging is not a technique that typically pays off for many beginner options traders because of its complexity. While the concepts of applying it are simple, the practical application is not. The options trader needs to be well-acquainted with the market and more basic options trading techniques before attempting this one. The trader needs to also be able to follow short-term trends in the financial market as well as be able to make correct calculations based on those trends. Then the trader needs to turn those calculations into fast decisions because legging is largely a technique that relies on timing and the transactions being applied in the right order.

The biggest risk is that the trader implements this technique at the wrong time and reduces his or her profits. Worse still, using legging ineffectively can lead to major losses. So while legging can indeed be a highly profitable technique, it can be disastrous if done wrong. The associated disadvantages include:

- Having the technique backfire on the options trader and lead to lowered profit margins
- Complete wipeout of profits
- Being legged out of a position that works for the trader.

Chapter Summary

The use of spreads, which is the purchase and sale of at least two different options with the same associate asset attached, is another tactical approach to options trading.

Credit spreads describe the selling of a high-premium option while purchasing a low-premium option in the same class. This results in a credit to the investor's account. Both of these options have the same expiration date but different strike prices. The aim here is to make a profit when the spread between the two options becomes narrowed.

On the other hand, a debit spread is one where the trader buys a high-premium option and sells a low-premium option with the same associated asset attached to both options. Just like with a credit spread, both options have the same expiration date but different strike prices. The trader makes a profit when the spread between the two options widen. This results in a debit to the trader's account.

The legging is a technique that allows for the multiple transactions associated with spreads. Every spread has two legs—the buying of one option and the selling of another. Normally these two transactions occur at the same time but there are instances where the trader separates the transactions. This process of separating the transactions is called legging.

The legging has several benefits that include:

- Preventing the loss due to several transactions being done at the same time.
- Facilitating a bigger profit by legging into or out of a certain position.
- The broker may be not in a position to carry out each transaction at the same time.
- The market climate may have changed and made it necessary to leg into another position for profitability's sake.
- Legging may be needed to lock in a profit or ensure losses stay to a minimum.

The legging needs to be done with caution because it can result in losses when not timed or ordered correctly.

Chapter 7:
Iron Condor

This options trading strategy is similar to the iron butterfly and has 4 transactions. The two strategies are mistaken for each other but the iron condor allows for a great profit margin. This is a result of the iron butterfly spread requiring the associated asset to be the same price to take maximum profit while the iron condor allows for a range to reach the profit margin. The downside of this is that the maximum profit that can be earned is lowered.

The particulars of the iron condor are:

Strategy type: Neutral

Trader Level: Advance

Spread type: Credit

This options strategy requires 4 transactions. The trader has to:

- Sell 1 out of the money put
- Buy 1 out of the money put (has the lower strike)
- Sell 1 out of the money call
- Buy 1 out of the money call (has the higher strike)

All four options have the same expiration date.

The maximum profit available from this options strategy is equal to the net credit that is received upon entering the contract. Profit is earned when the associated asset prices at the expiration date fall between the call and put that are sold. The formula to calculate this looks like this:

Net Premium Received - Commissions Paid = Profit

The loss experienced with this strategy is limited and non-directional because this strategy is comparative to combining a bear call spread and a bull put spread. Loss is calculated with this formula:

Width of the two Strike Prices - Net Premium Received + Commissions Paid = Loss

Unfortunately, the loss can be a lot higher than the profit with this strategy because it can occur either when the price of the associated asset falls at or below the lower strike of the put or if it rises above or is equal to the higher strike of the call.

There are 2 breakeven points. Breakeven is calculated with these formulas:

Strike Price of Short Call + Net Premium Received = Breakeven

Strike Price of Short Put - Net Premium Received = Breakeven

Benefits of the Iron Condor Spread

- The stock can go in any direction and the trader can still make a profit.
- This is a flexible strategy that allows for minimizing risk while still potentially earning the trader profits every month.
- Profit can be made with a broad range at the date of expiration.
- These are short-term contracts so profits can be realized in 3 months or less.
- The investor can make predeterminations of what the potential losses and profits can be before entering the contract.

Risks of the Iron Condor Spread

The biggest disadvantage of this strategy is its complexity. The 4 legs mean that this is a strategy that is best suited for advanced traders. This means that any trader who does not understand options on the level needed or understands the financial market stands to makes a loss if he or she implements this strategy incorrectly.

Chapter Summary

A great alternative to the iron butterfly spread, this options strategy is great if a trader is trying to gain a profit from having a neutral outlook. It has for legs, which look like this:

- Sell 1 out of the money put
- Buy 1 out of the money put (has the lower strike)
- Sell 1 out of the money call
- Buy 1 out of the money call (has the higher strike)

Maximum profit is achieved when the associated asset price at the expiration date falls between the call and put that is sold. This is a strategy best left to advanced options traders.

Chapter 8:
Selling Naked Options

Naked options are also called uncovered options and they contrast with covered options. Naked options are so-called because the seller of the option does not own the associated asset attached to that contract. This kind of selling is known as writing or shorting an option. This is a highly vulnerable position for the seller because not having ownership of the asset means that he or she needs to acquire the asset at the expiration date should the trader of the option decide to exercise the right of ownership. The seller of this type of option is not protected from price volatility. This is why this type of option is known as uncovered or naked—due to the high level of exposure the seller faces. The seller runs the risk of having a high loss margin.

Despite this vulnerability, selling a naked option has a variety of benefits that many traders and investors find attractive, especially since this vulnerability and volatility is built into the premium. If the investor decides to exercise the right to the option, acquiring the asset creates a short sell position in the seller's account. Naked options can be further broken down into call options and put options.

Naked Call Options

The naked call option is a bearish strategy where the object of the seller is to gain a premium payment and exit the agreement.

This type of option describes the seller of the call option having an obligation to sell the asset and having no right to back out if the buyer of the option decides to exercise the right to buy.

This type of agreement is entered into when the price of the asset is expected to fall at the expiration date.

Profit is calculated using this formula:

Premium Received – Costs of Trade = Profit

This profit is acquired if the price of the associated asset is less than the strike price at the date of expiration.

As mentioned earlier, there is a great potential for loss with this options strategy. In fact, the loss is potentially unlimited. It is calculated with this formula:

Price of Security – Strike Price of Short Call - Net Premium + Costs of Trade = Loss

Loss is experienced when the price of the associated asset goes above the strike price. This can clearly be disastrous because there is no ceiling for this. This is the reason why many brokers do not encourage the use of this options trading strategy, especially if physical commodities are associated.

Breakeven is calculated with this formula:

Short Call Strike Price + Premium Acquired = Breakeven

Naked Put Option

The naked put option is a bullish strategy that has the same objective as with the naked call option—to gain a premium payment and exit the agreement.

This type of option describes the seller of the call option having an obligation to buy the asset and having no right to back out if the buyer of the option decides to exercise the right to sell. This type of agreement is entered into when the price of the asset is expected to rise at the expiration date.

Profit is calculated using this formula:

Premium Received – Costs of Trade = Profit

This profit is acquired if the price of the associated asset is more than the strike price at the date of expiration.

Loss is potentially unlimited in this case as well and occurs when the price of the asset falls. It is calculated with this formula:

Strike Price of Short Put - Price of Security - Option Premium + Costs of Trade = Loss

Breakeven is calculated with this formula:

Short Put Strike Price - Premium Acquired = Breakeven

Elements of a Naked Option

While this is a risky strategy, the naked option can be accomplished with success. The seller just has to get the elements right. These elements are:

- **Timing.** The seller needs to be certain the price of the asset is unlikely to move when selling a naked option. Volatility is not the name of the game in naked options trading.
- **Short expiration date.** Volatility is less likely in the short term so naked options traders should not develop naked options with far off expiration dates.
- **Protection.** A naked options trader can try to protect himself or herself by taking cash in hand for put options and physical security for call options up until the expiration date. If not, the seller should exit before the expiration date.

Benefits of Naked Options

We have talked a lot about the risks involved with selling naked options but that is not to say that using this options strategy cannot be advantageous. The benefits include:

- Naked options allow the seller to leverage more positions without the expense of margin interest compared to covered options.
- The upfront costs are lower compared to using a covered strategy.
- The seller gets to keep the premium even if the option is not exercised.

Chapter Summary

Unlike a covered option, the naked option is one where the seller of the option does not own the associated asset attached to that contract. The seller aim is to gain the payment of the premium then exit. Therefore, this is a strategy that should only be implemented if the seller is fairly certain that the price of the asset will not move up until on or by expiration date.

This is a risky strategy to employ as it exposes the seller to unlimited loss because the option is not protected against price volatility and he or she will have to deliver the associated asset if the investor decides to exercise the right of the option.

Despite the risks, using naked options can be a powerful way to leverage more positions. The benefits include having a lower upfront cost compared to covered options and the fact that the seller gets to keep the premium payment no matter what direction the asset takes.

The elements that need to be considered for selling a naked option include timing, the expiration date, and the level of protection the seller has.

Chapter 9:
Rolling Out Options

The process of rolling out describes an expiring option being replaced with an identical option. Rolling out is a great strategy to manage a losing or a winning position. This management is facilitated by closing one option position then opening another option with a similar position with the same associated asset but varied terms.

Most times, traders use this strategy to adjust the strike price and the length of time the trader would like to hold a short or long position. This strategy is one that even a beginner needs to be aware of because any options trader who trades for an extended amount of time will encounter it at some point or the other. Rolling can be done in 3 ways. These ways are:

- Rolling up
- Rolling down
- Rolling forward

We will look at each individual rolling over the type below:

How to Roll Out an Option

Rolling Up

This method of rolling up involves closing one existing option position while opening a similar position with a higher strike price at the same time. The higher strike price is the reason for the name. This method is simple and can be done in both a short and a long position. In a short position, all the trader has to do is buy to close the existing position. In the long position, the trader needs to sell to close the existing position. The next step is opening a new position with the same associated asset and a higher strike price. From a short position, the trader needs to sell to a new position. From a long position, the trader needs to buy a new position.

The procedure remains the same regardless of whether it revolves around a put or a call option. The result is different though for put and call options. If the trader rolls up a put option, the contract becomes more expensive thus the need for a higher strike price. If the trader rolls up a call option, the contract becomes less expensive. Therefore, the higher the strike price for a rolled up call option, the less expensive it becomes.

The effect is also affected by whether or not the put or call option is long or short. Rolling up a long put position entails selling cheaper options to make up the existing position so that the buying of more expensive options can be facilitated. On the other hand, rolling up short positions entails closing that position by buying cheaper options than writing up more expensive options.

Rolling up a long call position entails selling one position to enter into a cheaper one. This results in a profit. On the other hand, rolling up a short position means buying back cheaper options to write up new options with higher strike prices.

Rolling up options is done for a variety of reasons and is dependent on the trader's existing position and what circumstances surround that current position. One example where this might be a useful technique to employ is a situation where a contract is written up against stock that a trader already owns. If the price of the stock increases unexpectedly before the expiration date, the trader can roll up the option at a higher strike price that is out of money to prevent him or her from having to sell the stock.

Rolling up options is a useful strategy indeed. However, it does come with its own unique set of risks. Those risks become particularly high in volatile markets or in markets that are moving quickly in one particular direction. The changes in strike price between closing one position and entering another position can be detrimental if market value fluctuates at a high level.

There is another risk that goes by the name of slippage. Slippage is the circumstance that results when there is a time delay between two related options. This results in a price change during that time. This is a problem that many options traders face when they engage in multiple transactions that relate to one overall position. This is a problem that is particularly experienced when traders employ the use of spreads to gain multiple positions. This can be quite complex if the options trader is involved in several transactions at the same time.

Experienced traders become apt at handling this, though. To turn this problem around, the trader needs to roll up a specific transaction to close the existing position while opening up a new one at a higher strike price at the same time. Due to the complexity of this type of strategy, this is not recommended for a beginner to try.

Rolling Down

Rolling down is the method that involves closing one existing position while opening a similar position with a lower strike price at the same time. It is the opposite of rolling up. It can be applied to both puts and calls, and both short and long positions. The reasons for using this method typically revolves around the trader's current circumstance and the position that he or she is in.

The first reason that he or she might use rolling down is to prevent exercising on a short put position so that the obligation of having to buy the associated asset is avoided. Next, the trader might use rolling down to minimize losses on calls while still maintaining speculation on the associated asset recovering its value. Even though the expiration date may approach, the trader may maintain the belief that the price of the associated asset will increase again and therefore, use rolling down to buy a call at a lower strike price. This provides impact protection and betters chances of getting a profit if the associated asset does indeed climb in value as speculated.

Lastly, rolling down is a consideration for many options traders because they would like to make a profit off-put options while still holding a position whereby they can speculate that there will be further downward movement of the associated asset value. In this situation, the trader rolls down so that he or she can purchase puts with lower strike prices to benefit further from the fall in the associated asset's value. This allows for continued profit without risking the profit that has already been made.

Rolling Forward

There are many options that an options trader can exercise when open positions are approaching the expiration date if the maximum profit is not yet realized but is still probable, and one of those options is rolling forward. Rolling forward involves moving an open position to a different expiration date so that the length of the contract is extended. In essence, this is closing an existing position and opening a corresponding position based on the same option characteristics with a different expiration date. This is also known as rolling over.

This can be done by closing the existing position and entering a new one or entering a new position and then closing the existing one. As you can see, these as separate transactions and as such this is a form of a legging.

There are 2 common reasons why rolling forward is used by options traders. The first reason is that the trader may have taken a certain position expecting to profit in a greater way in the short-term but realizes after that a bigger profit will be realized over a longer period. The extension of the expiration date enables the trader to continue to profit from the option.

The second reason is that the trader may have entered into a position expecting the associated acid to move in a particular direction within a certain amount of time and later realized that this will take longer than expected. Extending the length of the contract allows the trader to profit from the contract at a later date.

The Benefits of Rolling Out

- Commission fees are lower because rolling out is conducted on one transaction rather than multiple.
- Rolling out allows the trader to save and thus, keeps more money in the pocket.
- The risk of slippage is reduced because the closing and opening of options positions are done simultaneously and not as separate transactions.
- Rolling over is a relatively simple strategy compared to other options trading strategies.

Chapter Summary

Rolling out options describes the process of an expiring option being replaced with an identical option. Rolling out is a great strategy to manage a losing or a winning position. It is facilitated by closing one option position then opening another option with a similar position with the same associated asset but varied terms like the adjustment of the strike price and the length of time the trader would like to hold a short or long position.

Rolling can be done in 3 ways. These ways are:

- Rolling up, which involves closing one existing option position while opening a similar position with a higher strike price at the same time.
- Rolling down, which involves closing one existing position while opening a similar position with a lower strike price at the same time.
- Rolling forward, which involves moving an open position to a different expiration date so that the length of the contract is extended.

The benefits of rolling over include:

- Lower commission fees.
- Increased trader savings.
- Reduced risk of slippage.
- The ease of transaction is suitable for beginners.

Chapter 10:
Top Trader Mistakes to Avoid in Options Trading

As a new options trader, it is very common to easily feel overwhelmed or overzealous in your pursuit of this business. Even though the risks of such a business are relatively low, making mistakes can be very costly. This chapter is dedicated to increasing the awareness of common mistakes that are made by beginners (and sometimes by advanced traders) so that you can avoid them with practical approaches.

Mistake #1—Not Having a Trading Plan to Fall Back On

Unfortunately, many people enter the arena of options trading out of desperation or greed with no plan as to how they will make this a successful venture. They are looking to make a quick buck and do not think things through because they are not thinking rationally. This leads to them trading with their emotions rather than with logic.

There is no place for emotions and feelings in options trading. While gut instinct has a time and a place in options trading, being led by anger, sadness, and other emotions can lead to heavy financial losses.

As this book has shown, many factors need to be considered if an options trader wants to make maximum profit. Therefore, going in half-cocked, desperate, or greedy will only lead to failure and unnecessary losses. To make the best out of this business venture you need to have a sound trading plan before you do a single thing. Your trading plan will serve as your comprehensive decision-making guide for all your trading activities.

Developing this plan relies on asking several questions, which include but are not limited to:

- What are your goals?
- How much time will you commit to options trading?
- Which financial markets do you want to trade-in?
- What strategies will you use to find opportunities in the financial market?
- How much capital do you have available to dedicate to options trading?
- How much are you willing to risk for every trade?
- What determines this risk?
- What are your risk management rules?
- When will you enter the trading market?
- What strategies will you implement to minimize your losses?
- What is your exit plan?
- How will you maintain a record-keeping system?

To answer these questions effectively, you need to take your emotions out of it and use your logical brain. Developing this plan is the only thing that will keep you moving forward and facilitate improvement as an options trader. With your plan finalized, you will realize that there is predictability and repeatability in options trading. Realizing these trends can help you maximize your profit by taking advantage of these features.

Mistake #2—Choosing the Wrong Expiration Date for Options

Having expiration dates that are too short or too long can be costly. While you develop your trading plan, you will definitely come across the factor of how you will select expiration dates for your options. Each option is unique and this requires setting up a system whereby you can select proper expiration dates so that profits are maximized every time.

When developing your options for choosing an expiration date, relying on a simple checklist system can help. Here are a few questions that you can add to this checklist so that you choose the best expiration date for that particular transaction:

- How long is this trade likely to play out?
- Does this timeline align with my own goals?
- Do I have adequate liquidity in the timeline to support my trade for the duration of the contract?
- What is the historical and implied volatility of the financial market?
- Have I factored in the Greeks like delta and theta?
- How will my particular strategy relate to time decay and profitability?

Mistake #3—Not Factoring In the Volatility of the Financial Market

Even the most stable financial markets can have days where they take off in an unexpected direction. This affects the value of the associated asset and so the options trader needs to be aware of this. Some traders only look at the reactivity of the financial markets during one period and not others and so do not rely on historic data or focus on forecasting the future. These are costly mistakes.

Ensure that the factoring of the market and stock volatility are always a consideration, even after the option has been finalized. Volatility in the market is inevitable. Look at the stock market and you will see how quickly it moves up and down over the short term. It is important you do not get carried away with short-term fluctuations. Know your strategy before you invest so that you are not distracted by short-term fluctuations.

While it is best to try to avoid volatility as much as possible when trading options, if you do decide to go the opposite route, limit your orders and ensure that you have a sound exit strategy.

Mistake #4—Not Having a Sound Exit Plan

This is a trading strategy that many novice options skip in their eagerness to get started. While they may have a strategy in place for entering options trading, they forget or are ignorant of the fact that an exit strategy is just as important.

One of the biggest reasons for developing an exit strategy is to prevent emotions from clouding your judgment during that time when tough decisions need to be made. As a result, make the plan before things hit the fan to take out that emotional aspect.

Two factors need to be considered when creating an exit plan for an option. They are:

- What is the absolute point you will get out of the trade if things are not working out in your favor?
- How will you take profits if things are working in your favor?

Many experienced options traders place a percentage cap on the trade to know at which point they will back out of the trade if things are not working out successfully for them. While it is normal for the value of the transaction to fluctuate between 10% and 20%, most experienced traders will cut their losses if their fluctuation goes between 30% and 50%.

This fluctuation needs to be considered also if things are working out in your favor. If the transaction has increased in value between 30% and 50%, you need to be thinking about how you can protect your profits or how to ensure that you do not lose any money through that option.

Your exit strategy can also be time-based. You may decide that pursuing a certain option is only worthwhile for you for a certain period and not beyond.

Having a target profit can also be the foundation of your exit strategy.

Mistake #5—Not Being Flexible

Never say never with options trading. Many traders get stuck in their ways when it comes to options trading and refuse to try out new strategies. Remember that having a growth mindset is necessary for success in any part of life and this philosophy also applies to options tradings.

You have to be willing to keep in the know when it comes to options and also be willing to learn and try new strategies. That does not mean try any strategy you come across. It simply means that when you do come across new strategies, assess them carefully to see if they have the potential to fit into your trading plan to help you accomplish your goals.

Mistake #6—Trading Illiquid Options

Liquidity describes how quickly an asset can be converted to cash without a significant price shift. The more readily the asset can be traded, the more liquid it is. Having a liquid market means there are ready and willing active buyers and sellers.

Highly liquid options have certain characteristics. Being high in volume is one such characteristic. The higher the volume of options, the easier they are to enter and exit. Having the ability to move in and out of a contract is a huge advantage to an options trader. Being easily adjustable is another characteristic. Seeking out option with these characteristics makes the job of an options trader that much easier

Examples of highly liquid assets attached to options include stock and ETFs.

On the other hand, there are illiquid options and establishing such a contract is a mistake that many novice options traders make. There are not easily moved or converted into cash. They drive up the cost of doing business because of this characteristic. This makes the trading cost higher and thus, this cuts on the trader's profits.

To avoid this, trade options that are higher in liquidity. For example, stocks that trade less than 1 million shares per day are liquid. Pursue such options at the beginning of your career as an options trader. Also, seek options with a greater volume and that are easily adjustable.

Mistake #7—Not Factoring In Upcoming Events

Of course, the financial market is volatile and unpredictable. Some things cannot be foreseen. However, others can be foreseen and it is the job of the options trader to keep these things in his or her foresight.

There are two major common events that an options trader needs to know in advance and these things are the earnings (the measure of how much a company's profits is allocated to each share of stock) on the associated assets as well as the dividend payout dates in these assets if they apply. Not knowing these future events can mean losing out on extra payout like these because no action was made to ensure that the trader had a right to them.

In the case of dividends, payment on the associated assets could have been collected by the trader if only he or she had the foresight to purchase that asset before those payments were processed.

To ensure you get such extra earning, you need to be on the ball of the date of such events. Do not sell options that have pending dividends and avoid trading in the earning season to avoid the common high volatility associated with that time.

Mistake #8—Waiting Too Long To Buy Back Short Strategies

You need to always be ready to buy back short strategies early in the game. Never assume that profits will continue to come in just because you are having a good period. The market can change any time and so your profits can be lost easily if you fail to react correctly.

There are many reasons why some options traders wait to do this and they include not wanting to pay commissions, trying to gain more profits out of the contract, and thinking that the contract will be worthless upon expiration. Thinking in such a manner is a mental trap that can lead to financial losses.

To avoid this, consider buying back your short strategies as long as you can keep at least 80% of your initial gain from the sale of that option. If you enter an out of money positions, reduce the risk by buying back.

Mistake #9—Getting Legged Out Of Position

Legging out means that one leg of the option closes out and essentially becomes worthless to the trader. The leg gains an unfavorable price that does not benefit the trader. This does not automatically spell the death of the option made up of several legs but it can expose the trader to loss.

Legging can be performed in several types of options including straddles, strangles, and spreads. These types of options can be enhanced by multiple legs and gain the options trader a leg up. However, the complexity of using the legging technique can elude even experienced options traders. The timing and order of executing legs make this a delicate process that needs a fine eye for the market. Therefore, this is a technique that must be attempt only after a trader is confident in his or her experience, knowledge, and success rate.

Mistake #10—Trading Options on Complicated Assets without First Doing Proper Research

In their overexcitement, many new traders like to go for complex assets because they believe that this where the big bucks are. Even if this is true in some cases, if the trader does not have a good grasp of how the asset works in its market, then he or she will fail to implement the right strategies to gain profits. Never just jump into an option. Do your research first. Also, as a newbie options trader, it might be best to get your feet wet with more common options rather than jumping into the deep end of the pool.

Chapter Summary

Trading options effectively relies on setting up systems that promote growth and improvement in the arena. But many people skip developing systems in their eagerness to get started. This can be very costly in many ways.

Please avoid the following mistakes when trading options. They are commonly made by beginners and can be very costly.

1. Not having a trading plan
2. Choosing the wrong expiration date
3. Not factoring in the volatility of the financial market
4. Not having an exit plan
5. Not being flexible
6. Trading illiquid options
7. Not factoring in upcoming events such as the date of dividend payments
8. Waiting too long, but to back short strategies
9. Legging into spreads
10. Trading options on complicated assets without first doing proper research

Chapter 11:
The Options Trader Mindset

A successful options trader is a unique individual. This person learns how to leverage their financial position to pave a way to profitable returns that make the time and effort invested worth it. This person is strong-willed and determined.

I have tried to break down the concepts in this book as simple as possible so that anyone can do it. The truth is even though everyone can understand these concepts and maybe the ability to implement these strategies, not everyone has the fortitude to stick with it until they gain the results they want—which is financial freedom. The people that do, fall into a small bracket. A strong options trader requires a unique set of skills, attitude, and persona.

The Traits of a Successful Options Trader

- **Being self-disciplined.** I am sure after reading this book, you may be excited about the possibility of gaining financial freedom by using options trading. If you are willing to jump with both feet in, I applaud you. I also implore you to exercise caution and therefore, self-discipline. Do not just stop your education on options with this book. Do more extensive research so that you can identify the best opportunities for you. Doing this will allow you to form the best strategy for your case and goals. Do not skip doing your homework because you are eager. Jumping the gun has led to many traders losing out. You need to rule your desires, wants, and actions rather than being ruled by them.
- **Being Committed.** A successful options trader is one that does not give up. He or she does not trade on an

on-again, off-again basis. This person is committed to the cause of building their financial success in this way and persists in their effort. Remember, I stated in the introduction of this book, that this is not a hobby. This is something you embrace as a business and part of your lifestyle. Go hard or go home. Options trading has no room for being tentative.

- **Continually learning.** The financial market is continuously evolving. It changes every single day. A successful trader needs to be able to roll with the punches and have a clear understanding of what is happening now. He or she needs to be able to make forecasts about the future as well. Continuously learning about the market also allows you to see new opportunities where amateur traders will not. One of the best ways to increase your knowledge of options is to follow the action of an experienced options trader. The point is not to copy his or her moves. Rather, it is to watch a master at work so that you can develop your own style of trading.
- **Being patient.** This relates to jumping the gun. You need to carefully weigh your options before you make a move while trading options. While there are risks involved in trading options, the market typically provides signs of these opportunities if a trader knows where and how to look. Control your emotions and strategize your entry into the trade market as well as your exit from trades.
- **Being an effective risk manager.** There is no guarantee when you trade options and as such, an effective options trader needs to be able to exploit his or her position to try to determine where he or she should take appropriate measures to capitalize on his or her gain. Part of managing risks involves being able to diversify your portfolio so that all your eggs are not in

one basket. A successful trader does not go chasing after every available option. Neither does he or she get stuck chasing China eggs that do not yield gain. Even though there is no guarantee that it will all work out, being able to effectively manage risks significantly lowers the chances of the loss happening.

- **Being able to manage money effectively**. The trader also needs to know how much capital should be allocated for trading. Throwing your money at all options will not lead to effective results. Actually, this is a recipe for losing money. Part of being a good money manager means the trader needs to be good with numbers so that he or she can calculate the vega, theta, delta, and gamma of their trade options, for example.
- **Maintaining accurate records.** This will help with decision-making and allows you to allocate your money effectively as you will have a history of your options within easy reach. My suggestion is that you do this digitally for easy access, better storage, and better organization. Digitally record-keeping also allows for the use of specialized software that makes life a lot simpler than looking through hard copies when records are needed.
- **Being an effective planner.** While there is a level of relying on instinct in trading options, you also need to have a plan so you do not place random trades. You need to have the direction to effectively move forward with obtaining financial freedom no matter which option you choose to do that. Having smart goals allow you to develop this plan. You also need to have a plan to cover any losses that may happen and a plan for how you can leverage the profit that you do make. Your plan needs to allow for flexibility and the great thing is that you can upgrade, downscale, and change the plan completely if need be.

- **Being able to accept losses gracefully.** The nature of the financial market is unpredictable and every trader makes a loss at some point. Having an apt understanding of the market will minimize this loss but you also need to be able to be flexible in how you handle this so that you do not get blindsided nor do you let this weigh you down. Remember that any successful person needs to be able to find a lesson in their failure so that they come back stronger and better in the future.

Dream Big

Many people are stuck in a state of financial dependency and insecurity because they do not see themselves being any better than they are now. Therefore, they never take any actions or risks to elevate themselves

You need to be able to visualize your success to manifest it. To develop yourself into a brilliant trader, you need to be able to see yourself in the future as a successful entrepreneur who implemented a plan to gain passive income and is, therefore, able to enjoy the freedom of using your time as you see fit.

The brain has a way of manifesting action to make what it sees a reality so use that to your advantage. See yourself as a successful options trader today. Imagine the way that you would look, the way that you would feel, how you would dress and everything else that being an options trader means to you. See yourself being more than what you are today no matter your current circumstances. Do not place any limits on yourself.

The mistake that many options traders make at the beginning is that they think small. They imagine maybe making a few hundred dollars here and there to subsidize their current lifestyle. They make that the pinnacle of their success even though many options traders make hundreds of thousands and millions of dollars every day.

The people that dream so small have their own reasons but a common reason is that they do not want to be too disappointed if things do not work out. This way of thinking is limiting and self-fulfilling. You are stopping yourself from achieving greatness and reaching your true potential with such a mindset. Instead, you have to dream big, bold dreams. It is the only thing that will keep you motivated in tough times. You have to *know* that you can do this and make this a successful business no matter the odds.

I know that at the beginning, it may be tough especially when people laugh at your dreams of becoming a success. Remember that you are not doing this for them. Those people may be your friends and family and of course, this hurts. Do not allow this to demotivate you. Keep strong and remember that you are doing this for you, not them. If you need to, make it an extra motivator to prove them wrong. Give yourself the last laugh.

Visualizing allows you to have something to work towards. The vision creates a hunger within you to manifest that picture in your mind into reality. It builds anticipation and creates excitement. It gives you a sense of purpose. Allow yourself to be consumed by that passion.

My belief is that every person on this planet is capable of doing great things so stop limiting yourself. Stop underestimating your potential. One of the most significant attributes of an options trader is being able to follow his or her gut. You will never develop that knack for trading options if you continually doubt yourself and your purpose.

All of the traits that are stated above are things that can be learnt. So it is fine if you have not developed these traits as yet. The point is to make it a habit to develop them starting today. The first thing you need to do is picture yourself as the successful options trader that you will be in the future. Then put in the work to make that vision a reality.

Chapter Summary

A successful options trader is a special individual. This person has a special group of traits that include:

- Being self-disciplined
- Been committed
- Continuously seeking learning
- Being patient
- Being an effective risk manager
- Being good at numbers
- Maintaining accurate records
- Effectively planning and being flexible.

As great as these traits are to any options trader who aims for success, the first thing any beginner needs to do is dream big enough to achieve that success. If your mindset is limiting you, you will never be a master options trader or someone who is financially free. There are no limits to what an options trader can achieve so stop limiting yourself with your mindset.

Chapter 12:
Trading with LEAPS

The acronym LEAPS stands for Long-term Equity Anticipation Securities. They are a type of option with expiration dates that are longer than normal. They last for at least 1 year and sometimes go as far as 3 years into the future. As mentioned earlier, the expiration dates of options are typically a few months into the future. The typical option expiration ranges are 3 months, 6 months, and 9 months.

This is because options are typically a short term way of investing.

LEAPS step away from the norm and have a longer shelf-life compared to your average option. They still possess the qualities as a normal option. LEAPS appeal to investors that want a long-term investment without being obliged by that investment. It also appeals to the investor who is anticipating a profitable yield from a particular market in the future but does not have the capital at hand to make that substantial investment. They are more affordable than such assets like stock because, despite the longer expiration date, they are still options and thus, stick to option price ranges. LEAPS normally have a slightly higher price than other short term contracts

LEAPS have a seat at the options table because sometimes the value of the associated asset needs more time to appreciate. Typical options expire in a few months. These options can yield profits in a short amount of time but there is also the risk that the transaction might not be as profitable if the stock or other associated asset does not move significantly up or down.

LEAPS are the solution that allows the time for appreciation of the associated asset. A trader can even extend the expiration on that LEAP option with another LEAP if the time period is still too short for the asset to reach profitability. For example, a LEAP with an expiration date of 2 years can be held for 1 year then be sold to replace it with a 3-year expiration date. This is called rolled LEAPS.

Rolling the option forward is normally relatively inexpensive because it still carries the same characteristics. Other factors can become unpredictable, though. Such factors include interest rates, dividends, and volatility.

The question that stumps many traders about LEAPS is whether to use a call option or a put option. The answer to that is dependent on whether the trader expects a bullish or bearish price movement. If the trader believes that the associated asset is bullish by the expiration date, he or she should buy call options. If instead he or she believes that the associated asset will drop in value by the expiration date, then the trader should buy put options.

Best Strategies for Using LEAPs

Some strategies work best when it pertains to LEAPS and this list includes:

- **Long call.** This involves the purchase of LEAPS call options in anticipation of a long term bullish trend in the market.
- **Long put.** This involves the purchase of LEAPS put options in anticipation of a long term bearish trend in the market.
- **Rolling LEAPS options.** As mentioned earlier, this involves selling the LEAPS before expiration date while buying LEAPS with similar characteristics with at least 2-year expiration dates at the same time.

- **Bull call spread.** This options strategy is considered to reduce the initial cost of buying a call option. This can help offset the higher cost of LEAPS compared to standard options. Only use this strategy if you are confident that there will be a moderate rise in the price of the stock to send it up to the strike price.
- **Bull call spread.** This is another strategy meant to offset the higher cost of LEAPs. It is a bearish strategy. Profits are earned when the stock prices fall.
- **Calendar call spread.** This strategy is meant for a trader who wishes to benefit from the associated assets staying stagnant in the market while also benefiting from the long-term call position if the stock becomes more valuable in the future.

Benefits of LEAPS

LEAPS have several benefits and they include:

- LEAPS are sustainable as they allow a trader to piggyback off-market trends. This allows the trader to observe the movement of stock prices and have an option to buy or sell without making the full commitment of ownership.
- LEAPS are less volatility and so offer greater security. A trader who enters into such an option is looking at a stock that is increasing or decreasing in price over the long haul. This allows the trader the time to really ponder on the profitability of pursuing the asset. This person can use data offered over that time such as the current trends, news, and terms to base their future decision.
- LEAPS can serve great security in your financial portfolio as well as provide shareholders with a greater grip of the stock.

- LEAPS allow time for improvisation because the expiration date is longer.
- Buying LEAPS is cheaper than buying several standard options back to back.

Disadvantages of LEAPS

There are two sides to every coin. So, just as LEAPS are beneficial, there are also a few downsides. The first disadvantage of LEAPS is the strike price. Because they are priced higher, the trader needs to see movement in the asset price to gain a profit in addition to it taking longer for the option holder to breakeven.

The longer expiration dates on LEAPS make them less predictable. Therefore, pricing correctly so that a return is seen without the transaction being too costly is made can be difficult. Lastly, the trader will not benefit from any attached dividends or stock repurchase.

LEAPS are also sensitive to implied volatility and so, can lower in value when implied volatility drops.

Tips for Getting the Most Out Of LEAPS

- Pretend as if you are investing. This allows you to search for assets that you are interested n and maybe already have some know-how about. This makes it a lot easier to keep up-to-date with market trends compared to if you do not know anything about the asset and are not interested in learning more.
- Make use of the long expiration date. The benefits of the longer expiration date have been stated so ensure that these work to your benefit.
- Choose LEAPS that are more liquid.

- Prepare for the fact that LEAPS are more volatile than stocks but less volatile than standard options.
- Set targets for the stock prices in comparison to your LEAPS. Knowing those targets will allow the trader to sell at the most profitable time.
- Have an exit strategy in case the option is not working out according to plan.
- Always be aware of your position and be prepared to leverage it. Even though the expiration date is far off, you need to keep abreast as to whether the market is playing out as you anticipated. You need to be aware of the fluctuations in the asset's price. This will allow you to decide that makes this transaction the most profitable it can be for you. You can implement strategies like rolling the option forward and selling the first option as a loss so that you can move to another strike price that benefits you more.

Chapter Summary

LEAPS stands for Long-term Equity Anticipation Securities. This is an option that has an expiration date that is at least 1 year, which is a deviation away from the standard short options that carry expiration dates that are only a few months. LEAPS are a great option for a long term investor who wants to experiment with options without having to be apprehensive about the volatility of the financial market in the short term. LEAPS are also a great way for investors who do not have a great amount of capital available to them at present to enter into the market with lowered risk.

This long term maturity does have many benefits such as being sustainable, more secure, and not being subject to the decay of time. However, there are disadvantages as well, like the option being higher priced than standard options, being less predictable because of the far off timeline, and taking longer to breakeven compared to a standard option.

To get the most out of trading LEAPS, the trader needs to be strategic. Tips like staying abreast of market trends despite having a longer expiration date, having an exit plan if things go left field, and be prepared to leverage your position will help the trader gain maximum profit.

Conclusion

Financial freedom is an elusive thing but it is still attainable to any and everyone is willing to put in the time and effort to learn how to gain that freedom. Most people remain stuck financially because they do not see a way out. Even more unfortunate is that many people do not realize that they are bound by financial slavery. However, the only sign that you need to see to know that you are a financial slave is that you are unable to use your time in the way that you would like because you are trading this time for money actively. If you depend on one source of income such as a job just to survive then you are a financial slave.

The great news is that this does not have to be your reality indefinitely.

Trading Options for Financial Freedom

One of the leading ways of gaining financial freedom is setting up passive income streams. Trading options have the potential to be a powerful form of passive income. Not only does this activity give the trader the platform to gain financial freedom but it also allows the trader to pursue hobbies, career options, and other activities that he or she loves. It allows this because the trader is not actively trading time for money. Options traders have the flexibility to live and work anywhere in the world because, when done right, trading options allow the trader to earn tens of thousands of dollars and even more while he or she sleeps.

This book was written as a comprehensive guide to show that any and everyone can earn a sizable income from options trading as long as this person is willing to develop a growth mindset, learn from the mistakes and successes of other traders and work to put in that human and financial investment upfront. Options are derivative contracts that allow the owner of the contract the right to buy or sell the associated asset by an expiration date specified. From this definition, you can see that this is not something you simply dabble in now and then.

Are You Ready To Be An Options Trader?

Trading options is a business. Therefore, it needs to be approached with a mindset that is set for growth and development. We have talked about many topics on how you can get started such as developing your training plan, paper trading, opening a brokerage account, and choosing a trading style. All of these things plus learning the language of options trading is greatly important as a beginner in this field. You cannot get through into this career and profit in the way that you would like without putting in that initial study. This book should only be your starting point when it comes to learning. Gain more advice in the form of other books, online study, and from a mentor if possible.

After you have done this, you need to practically implement the strategies and techniques taught in this book. To remember what a put option and a call option are, you need to be able to see them in practice. To mentally solidify what a long position and a short position are, you need to actually be in these positions. To become familiar with volatility and interest rates, you need to put yourself in a position to learn further. Straddles, strangles, legging, debit spreads, credit spreads, selling naked options, and rolling out options... They might seem intimidating on paper and might be difficult to implement at first but practice makes perfect. All advanced options traders started as a beginner but a consistent, persistent effort took them to the next level.

This is a new world for any novice and, of course, it can seem intimidating but as long as you remained committed to developing the traits of a successful options trader, you will be well on your way to obtaining the financial freedom that you crave. Just as with any new venture, there will be setbacks and failures. You will lose your footing sometimes and be exposed to things that you never have been before. The keys to getting past all these things and overcoming your circumstances to gain success are being self-disciplined, being committed, being patient and, developing an eagerness for continual learning. You need to be an effective risk manager to juggle your options. You need to be able to manage your money effectively and keep accurate records that help you forecast your decisions based on sound history and knowledge. Most importantly, you need to dream big and stop limiting yourself. The sky is the limit with options trading. So stop settling for less than you deserve and visualize the future where you have ascertained that financial independence and stability. Then, do the work.

My Final Words

In closing, I would like to tell you that financial freedom is not given to most. It is built and developed with sound planning and execution of plans. You can see the truth in my words as most modern entrepreneurs who found great success did not come into this with a silver spoon in their mouths. Their success was not a gift from anyone else. Some of them even came from dismal circumstances such as homelessness to build a multi-billion dollar empire.

You have the same potential just like those other people did. You just have to be willing to put into the work to develop yourself, your state of mind, and a plan for creating the future that you would like rather than what a salary that does not support your desired lifestyle dictates. Yes, it might take some hard work to get your footing grounded with options trading but the payoff is more than worth it. Putting in the work upfront will allow you to gain the passive income that will allow you to pursue the other things that you would like to do with your time.

This book was written to show you that a lot of persons who are financially dependent on the broken system that society has made remain financially chained because of limited thinking. Open up your mind and visualize what you can accomplish. **Then get up and do it**. With the knowledge that you have found in this book, you can finally leave those shackles behind and create a future where you are financially free and happy. Good luck!

Mark Robert Rich

Glossary of Terms

To make your entry into the options trading world as easy as possible, I have provided an alphabetically ordered list of terms with the corresponding definition for easy reference. Please reference this section any time you need clarification on the jargon of options trading.

Active Income: The state whereby a person has to actively trade time for an income.

Asset: A property that is considered valuable and accessible to meet financial obligations and development.

At The Money: This means the asset price and the strike price are the same and so the options trader does not make a profit but neither does he or she make a loss on the transaction.

Basket Option: Options that use a group of securities as the asset associated with the contract.

Bear Call Spread: A bearish trading strategy for advanced options traders.

Bear Put Spread: A bearish trading strategy for beginner options traders.

Beta: A Greek measurement that helps predict stock volatility.

Bearish Outlook: Characterized by the decreasing value of the associated asset attached to an option.

Binomial Option Pricing Model: An options premium pricing model commonly used for pricing for American options.

Black Scholes Model: An options premium pricing model commonly used to price European options.

Breakeven: The state whereby a trader does not make a profit or loss from an option.

Bull Call Spread: A bearish trading strategy for beginner options traders.

Bull Put Spread: A bullish trading strategy for advanced options traders.

Bullish Outlook: Characterized by the rising value of the associated asset attached to an option.

Butterfly Spread: A neutral strategy for advanced traders.

Calendar Call Spread: This strategy is meant for a trader who wishes to benefit from the associated assets staying stagnant in the market while also benefiting from the long-term call position if the stock becomes more valuable in the future.

Call Options: This is the type of option that gives the trader the right to buy the asset on or before the expiration date.

Cash account: An account that is loaded with cash to facilitate the buying of options.

Commodity Options: Options that use physical commodity as the asset associated with the contract.

Covariance: A measure of a stock's sensitivity relative to that of the financial market.

Covered Call: This describes the act of selling the right to purchase a specified asset that you own at a specified price within a specified amount of time, which is usually less than 12 months. Also known as a buy-write.

Credit Spreads: This describes the selling of a high-premium option while purchasing a low-premium option in the same class (calls or puts).

Currency Option: Options that use the type of security grants the right to buy or sell a specific currency at a previously agreed-to exchange rate. Also referred to as a forex option.

Day Trading: A method of options trading involving trades that do not last more than a day as profits, losses, or breakeven are realized by the end of the day and so the options are closed.

Debit Spreads: This describes the buying of a high-premium option while selling a low-premium option with the same associated asset attached to both options.

Delta: A Greek that describes an option's sensitivity in relation to the price of the stock.

Derivative Contract: A contract that derives its value based on the value of the underlying asset.

Dividends: The distributions of portions of a company's profit at a specified period.

Earnings: The measure of how much a company's profits are allocated to each share of stock.

Emergency Fund: A reserve of cash or other assets developed to help navigate away from financial problems or unexpected financial pitfalls.

ETF: Exchange-traded fund.

Expiration Date: The date at which the option (contract) expires.

Financial Freedom: The ability to make decisions without being limited by finances.

Financial Independence: The state of having personal wealth to maintain the desired lifestyle and the standard of living wanted without having to trade daily hours for money.

Financial Security: The condition whereby a person supports their standard of living presently and in the future by having stable sources of income and other resources available.

Financial Slavery: The state of having decisions and opportunities limited by finances.

Fixed Mindset: A state of mind whereby a person believes that their qualities are fixed traits that cannot be changed.

Futures Option: Type of option that gives the trader the right to assume a certain position at a future date.

Gamma: A Greek that reflects the rate of change of the delta.

Greeks: A collection of degrees that provide a measure of an option's sensitivity in relation to other factors.

Growth Mindset: A state of mind whereby a person believes that their most basic abilities can be developed with hard work, continuous learning, and dedication.

Historical Volatility: This is a measure of how a stock has performed over the last 12 months.

Implied Volatility: This is a measure of how a stock will perform in the future.

In The Money: This means the asset price is above the call strike price and so the options trader makes a profit on the transaction.

Index: A measure of the stocks, bonds, and other securities a company possesses.

Index Options: Options that use a company's index as the asset associated with the contract.

Interest Rate: The percentage of a particular rate for the use of money lent over a period.

Intrinsic Value: The difference in the current price of an asset and the strike price of the option.

Iron Butterfly Spread: A neutral strategy for advanced options traders.

Iron Condor Spread: Neutral options strategy. Similar to the iron butterfly spread.

Lambda: A Greek that describes an option's sensitivity in relation to the associated asset's value.

LEAPS: The acronym stands for Long-term Equity Anticipation Securities. They are a type of option with expiration dates that are longer than normal.

Legging: The process of separating the individual transactions in an option.

Legging Out: One leg of the option closes out and becomes worthless to the options trader.

Liquidity: This describes how quickly an asset can be converted to cash without a significant price shift.

Long Call: This is an options strategy considered by options traders who want to make a profit from an asset that increases in the price above the strike price.

Long Position: The investor owns the asset associated with the option.

Long Put: This is a type of option that gives the trader the right to sell the associated asset at the strike price on or before the expiration date.

Long Straddle: This is a neutral position in options trading. Also known as the buy straddle.

Long Strangle: This is a neutral position in options trading. Also called the buy strangle.

Loss: The negative difference between the amount earned from an option and costs associated with that option.

Margin Account: An account that allows an options trader to borrow money against the value of the securities in the trader's account.

Market Makers: Options traders who ensure that the market is liquid and has transactions to be engaged in by buyers and sellers.

Market Volatility: This describes the rate at which prices change in any financial market.

Monte Carlo Simulations: An options premium pricing model that allows for considering multiple outcomes due to the involvement of random factors.

Options: A derivative contract that allows the owner of the contract to have the right to buy or sell the securities based on an agreed-upon price by a specified period.

Out Of the Money: This means the price is below the call strike price and so the options trader makes a loss on the transaction.

Naked Options: This is an option where the seller of the option does not own the associated asset attached to that contract.

Naked Call Option: A bearish options trading strategy.

Naked Put Option: A bullish options trading strategy.

Paper Trading: The act of practicing how to earn a profit from options trading on paper before investing actual money.

Passive Income: The state whereby a person earns income without the active input of time as an exchange.

Position Trading: This is a low-maintenance options trading style that introduces low risk but requires an advanced trader's knowledge and understanding of options and the financial markets.

Premium: The price paid by the buyer of the option.

Price Volatility: This describes how the price of an asset moves up or down.

Profit: The positive difference between the amount earned from an option and costs associated with that option.

Put Options: This is the type of option that gives the trader the right to sell the specified asset at the predetermined price by the expiration date.

Reverse Iron Butterfly: A volatile strategy for advanced traders.

Rho: A Greek that describes an option's sensitivity to the interest rate.

Rolling Down: This is the method that involves closing one existing position while opening a similar position with a lower strike price at the same time. It is the opposite of rolling up.

Rolling Forward: This involves moving an open position to a different expiration date so that the length of the contract is extended. Also known as rolling over.

Rolling LEAPS Options: This involves selling LEAPS before the expiration date while buying LEAPS with similar characteristics with at least 2-year expiration dates at the same time.

Rolling Out Options: The process of rolling out explains that an expiring option is replaced with an identical options.

Rolling Up: This involves closing one existing option position while opening a similar position with a higher strike price at the same time. It is the opposite of rolling down.

Securities: The assets attached to options. Examples include stock, currencies, and commodities.

Short Butterfly Spread: A volatility-based strategy that is typically practiced by medium to advanced options traders.

Short Position: The investor does not own the asset being associated with the option.

Short Straddle: This is a neutral options trading strategy. Also called a sell straddle.

Short Strangle: This is a neutral options trading strategy. Also called a sell strangle.

Slippage: This is the circumstance that results when there is a time delay between two related options, which results in a price change during that time.

Stock: A representation of shares of ownership in individual companies or options.

Stock Option: Options that use stock in a publically listed company as the asset associated with the contract.

Stock Volatility: A stock price's sensitivity to the financial market.

Straddles: This is an options trading strategy whereby the trader protects himself or herself regardless of if the price of the stock moves up or down.

Strangles: This is an options strategy employed when the trader strongly believes that the stock price will move either up or down but still wants to be protected in case he or she is wrong.

Strike Price: The price the trader strikes against the underlying value of the asset associated with the options to make a profit. Also called the agreed-upon price.

Swing Trading: A style of options trading that is particularly useful for part-time trading as well as beginners who are just getting the hang of things.

Theta: A Greek that describes an option's sensitivity in relation to how time affects the premium of an option.

Time value: The difference between the intrinsic value of an option and the premium.

Trading Plan: A comprehensive decision-making guide for an options trader.

Uncovered Call: A two-part strategy that describes the act of selling the right to purchase a specified asset that the investor owns at a specified price within a specified amount of time, which is usually less than 12 months. Also known as a buy-write.

Variance: A measure of how the market moves relative to its mean.

Vega: A Greek that measures an option's price sensitivity in relation to implied volatility.

Volatility: Describes how likely a price change will occur during a specified amount of time on the financial market.

From The Same Author

Stock Market Investing for Beginners

Complete Guide to the Stock Market with Strategies for Income Generation from ETF, Day Trading, Options, Futures, Forex, Cryptocurrencies and More
Rich M. R. (2020 april)

Day Trading Options

Most Complete Course for Beginners with Strategies and Techniques for Day Trading for a Living
Rich M. R. (2020 may)

www.ingramcontent.com/pod-product-compliance
Lightning Source LLC
Chambersburg PA
CBHW071414210526
45465CB00001B/388